S. Hrg. 113–439

ECONOMIC DEVELOPMENT: ENCOURAGING INVESTMENT IN INDIAN COUNTRY

HEARING

BEFORE THE

COMMITTEE ON INDIAN AFFAIRS
UNITED STATES SENATE

ONE HUNDRED THIRTEENTH CONGRESS

SECOND SESSION

JUNE 25, 2014

Printed for the use of the Committee on Indian Affairs

U.S. GOVERNMENT PRINTING OFFICE

90–934 PDF   WASHINGTON : 2014

For sale by the Superintendent of Documents, U.S. Government Printing Office
Internet: bookstore.gpo.gov   Phone: toll free (866) 512–1800; DC area (202) 512–1800
Fax: (202) 512–2104   Mail: Stop IDCC, Washington, DC 20402–0001

COMMITTEE ON INDIAN AFFAIRS

JON TESTER, Montana, *Chairman*
JOHN BARRASSO, Wyoming, *Vice Chairman*

TIM JOHNSON, South Dakota	JOHN McCAIN, Arizona
MARIA CANTWELL, Washington	LISA MURKOWSKI, Alaska
TOM UDALL, New Mexico	JOHN HOEVEN, North Dakota
AL FRANKEN, Minnesota	MIKE CRAPO, Idaho
MARK BEGICH, Alaska	DEB FISCHER, Nebraska
BRIAN SCHATZ, Hawaii	
HEIDI HEITKAMP, North Dakota	

MARY J. PAVEL, *Majority Staff Director and Chief Counsel*
RHONDA HARJO, *Minority Deputy Chief Counsel*

CONTENTS

ECONOMIC DEVELOPMENT: ENCOURAGING INVESTMENT IN INDIAN COUNTRY

WEDNESDAY, JUNE 25, 2014

U.S. SENATE,
COMMITTEE ON INDIAN AFFAIRS,
Washington, DC.

The Committee met, pursuant to notice, at 2:30 p.m. in room 628, Dirksen Senate Office Building, Hon. Jon Tester, Chairman of the Committee, presiding.

OPENING STATEMENT OF HON. JON TESTER, U.S. SENATOR FROM MONTANA

The CHAIRMAN. I call this hearing of the Senate Indian Affairs Committee to order.

Today we are going to hold an oversight hearing on Economic Development: Encouraging Investment in Indian Country. We all know how important economy is. According to the BIA, 50 percent of the folks over the age of 16 in Indian Country are unemployed.

Today we are going to look at what tools are out there, what resources are available, whether it is in energy, agriculture, tourism or manufacturing. We are going to look at the impacts of bureaucratic red tape on holding back economic development as well as the availability of capital and a number of other things that are very important to economic development in Indian Country.

I want to thank our panelists for being here today. What we are going to do, because we have votes at 2:30, so this is going to be kind of a screwed up hearing. We will get right to you, Mr. Nolan, and right to the testimony. Our first witness will discuss the programs with the U.S. Department of Treasury. Mr. Dennis Nolan is Deputy Director of the CDFI Fund, which was created to foster community development at financial institutions that provide access to capital to distressed and under-served communities, which includes much of Indian Country. While Mr. Nolan works with the CDFI Fund, I want to take a moment to express my appreciation for the Treasury's efforts on improving its relationship with Indian Country and the IRS for publishing a final rule on the general welfare exclusion doctrine. We thank you very much.

You may proceed, Mr. Nolan.

STATEMENT OF DENNIS NOLAN, ACTING DIRECTOR, COMMUNITY DEVELOPMENT FINANCIAL INSTITUTIONS, U.S. DEPARTMENT OF THE TREASURY

Mr. NOLAN. Good afternoon, Chairman Tester and distinguished members of the Senate Committee on Indian Affairs. My name is Dennis Nolan and I am the Acting Director of the Community Development Financial Institutions or CDFI Fund.

I am very pleased to have this opportunity to join you today and speak about the CDFI Fund's efforts to promote development in Indian Country. The CDFI Fund's work in Indian Country is born of an awareness that Native communities all across the Nation face extraordinary economic challenges and limited access to capital.

However, while the CDFI Fund is well aware that Native people continue to face daunting challenges, we also recognize that there is another story to be told about the economic life of Native communities, a story that is far more positive and far less widely reported. This story is one of progress. More and more Native communities are promoting sustainable economic that is fostering greater opportunities and transforming the lives of their people. I am proud to report that this story is one that the CDFI Fund is helping to write.

The CDFI Fund's commitment to serving Native communities has its origins in the creation of the CDFI Fund itself and is deeply rooted in the CDFI Fund's mission and vision. Soon after the CDFI Fund's creation, we began a comprehensive, multi-year study of lending and investment practices on Indian reservations and other land held in trust by the United States.

In 2001, the CDFI published the landmark Native American Lending Study. The study concluded that one of the key reasons for the lack of economic opportunity in Native communities was the lack of access to capital and financial services. The study identified 17 major barriers that limit access to capital in Native communities and offered a variety of recommendations to address them. Those recommendations became the blueprint for the CDFI's Native Initiatives.

The Native Initiatives has two main components. The first is the Native American CDFI Assistance Program, a funding program that provides financial assistance and technical assistance awards to build and expand the capacity of Native community development financial institutions, or Native CDFIs. Since it was launched in 2001, the Native American CDFI Assistance Program has provided awards totaling more than $93 million to help Native CDFIs deliver financial services and financial products to their communities.

What started as just a few Native CDFIs a ten years ago has grown to 68 Native CDFIs headquartered in 21 States.

The second component of the Native Initiatives is a series of training initiatives that further support the development of Native CDFIs. For example, we have recently launched part two of our training series called the Leadership Journey: Native CDFI Growth and Excellence. Between the Leadership Journey I and II, we provided over 2,000 hours of direct one-on-one capacity building efforts.

In addition to providing financial assistance and training for Native CDFIs, the CDFI Fund is committed to conducting comprehensive research to evaluate economic issues in Native communities. I mentioned the CDFI's Native Lending Study published in 2001. In 2013, we began working on a new lending study called Access to Credit and Capital in Native Communities, which will provide a detailed analysis to support new, actionable recommendations for improving access to capital and credit in Native communities.

The CDFI Fund has listed comments from Indian Country to help shape this new study and has conducted seven tribal consultations and numerous interviews with individuals at the local, regional and national level. The study examines such topics as financial education, Native entrepreneurship, housing, tribes and tribal enterprises and legal institutions, among others.

There is clear evidence about the CDFI program's economic development in Native communities. From 2004 to 2012, Native CDFIs made over 15,000 loans totaling $365 million in Native communities. Certified CDFIs made almost 7,000 loans and investments totaling $184 million in Native communities. Native CDFIs reported that their loans and investments created or retained more than 2,000 jobs. And new market tax credit program investments in Native communities totaled approximately $600 million.

While these are impressive statistics, we at the CDFI Fund believe that the true impact of our programs cannot be measured by the numbers alone, because our work is not just about creating programs and offering services. Our work and the work of every Native CDFI is about changing lives and building stronger, more resilient communities.

While we are mindful that these communities still face many challenges, we know that they are resourceful, resilient and capable because we have seen what can be accomplished. So we are more committed than ever to serving Native communities and extending access to capital to those places where access to opportunity is needed most.

On behalf of everyone at Treasury and the CDFI Fund, I would like to express our gratitude for the important work of this Committee and I look forward to working with you in the future.

Mr. Chairman, that concludes my formal statement. I will be happy to answer any questions.

[The prepared statement of Mr. Nolan follows:]

PREPARED STATEMENT OF DENNIS NOLAN, ACTING DIRECTOR, COMMUNITY DEVELOPMENT FINANCIAL INSTITUTIONS, U.S. DEPARTMENT OF THE TREASURY

Good afternoon, Chairman Tester, Vice Chairman Barrasso, and distinguished members of the Senate Committee on Indian Affairs. My name is Dennis Nolan, and I am the Acting Director of the Community Development Financial Institutions Fund (CDFI Fund). I am very pleased to have this opportunity to join you today and to speak about the CDFI Fund's efforts to promote economic development in Indian Country.

The CDFI Fund's work in Indian Country is born of an awareness that Native communities all across the nation continue to face extraordinary economic challenges that limit access to capital. However, while the CDFI Fund is well aware that Native people continue to face daunting challenges, we also recognize that there is another story to be told about the economic life of Native communities—a story that is far more positive and far less widely reported.

This story is one of progress. More and more Native communities are promoting sustainable economic development that is fostering greater opportunities and transforming the lives of their people.

I am proud to report that this story is one that the CDFI Fund is helping to write.

The CDFI Fund's Commitment to Native Communities

The CDFI Fund's commitment to serving Native communities has its origins in the creation of the CDFI Fund itself and is deeply rooted in the CDFI Fund's mission and vision.

The CDFI Fund was established by Congress with the passage of the Riegle Community Development and Regulatory Improvement Act of 1994, a bipartisan initiative. Our mission is to promote economic development in disadvantaged communities throughout the United States. We accomplish that goal not by providing direct funding to individuals or projects, but by certifying and providing financing and capacity-building services to non-governmental entities called Community Development Financial Institutions or CDFIs.

CDFIs are specialized financial institutions dedicated to serving low-income communities. There are several different types of CDFIs, including loan funds, community development banks, credit unions, and venture capital funds. All of them have the primary mission of serving communities and individuals that lack access to credit and other financial services from mainstream financial institutions.

Soon after the CDFI Fund's creation, we began a comprehensive multi-year study of lending and investment practices on Indian reservations and other land held in trust by the United States. In 2001, the CDFI Fund published the landmark *Native American Lending Study*.[1] The *Study* concluded that one of the key reasons for the lack of economic opportunity in Native communities was the lack of access to capital and financial services. The Study identified 17 major barriers that limit access to capital in Native communities and offered a variety of recommendations to address them. Those recommendations became the blueprint for the CDFI Fund's Native Initiatives.

The Native Initiatives have two main components. The first is the Native American CDFI Assistance Program (NACA Program), a funding program that provides financial assistance and technical assistance awards to build and expand the capacity of Native CDFIs. Financial assistance awards, used primarily for financial capital, are available only to entities that have been certified as Native CDFIs. In contrast, technical assistance grants are available to certified Native CDFIs, emerging Native CDFIs, and sponsoring entities. Sponsoring entities are unique to the NACA Program. Usually tribes or tribal entities, sponsoring entities create and support fledgling Native organizations as they move toward CDFI certification. Technical assistance grants are often used to acquire products or services including computer technology, staff training, and professional services such as market analysis, and support for other general capacity-building activities.

Since it was launched in 2001, the NACA Program has provided awards totaling more than $93 million to help Native CDFIs deliver financial services and financial products to their communities. What started as just a few Native CDFIs ten years ago has now grown to 68 Native CDFIs headquartered in 21 states. This growth was provided with extra support following the financial crisis when Congress waived the matching funds requirement for financial assistance awards from fiscal year 2009–2013.

The second component of the Native Initiatives is a series of training initiatives that further support the development of Native CDFIs. For example, we have recently launched Part II of a training series called *The Leadership Journey: Native CDFI Growth & Excellence*. The highly successful first part of the program provided training to 16 experienced Native CDFIs. Part II builds upon that success and offers a new cohort of 13 Native CDFIs in-person training events, along with continuous customized technical assistance, executive coaching, and peer mentoring over two years. Between The *Leadership Journey* I and II, we have provided over 2,000 hours of direct one-on-one capacity building efforts.

In addition, we have created a resource bank on our website that makes training curricula and reference materials used in a number of our training programs available to all Native CDFIs at no cost. Materials from Part II of *The Leadership Journey* series will be added to the resource bank as well, so even more Native CDFI leaders will have access to this outstanding training program.

In addition to providing financial assistance and training for Native CDFIs through the NACA Program, the CDFI Fund is committed to conducting comprehensive research to evaluate economic issues in Native communities. I mentioned the CDFI Fund's *Native American Lending Study*, published in 2001. In 2013, we began working on a new lending study called *Access to Capital and Credit in Native Communities*, which will provide detailed analysis to support new, actionable recommendations for improving access to capital and credit in Native communities. The

---

[1] *Study: http://www.cdfifund.gov/docs/2001*nactallendinglstudy.pdf.

CDFI Fund has solicited comments from Indian Country to help shape this new study, and has conducted seven tribal consultations and numerous interviews with individuals and local, regional, and national Native organizations. The study will examine such topics as financial education, Native entrepreneurship, housing, tribes and tribal enterprises, and legal institutions, among others. We expect the study to be completed by the end of 2014.

I will briefly mention two other CDFI Fund programs that are helping Native communities.

In 2013, we launched our new CDFI Bond Guarantee Program, an innovative initiative designed to inject substantial, long-term capital into our nation's most distressed communities, including Native communities. We are working closely with Native organizations to identify financial structures that will enable the CDFI Bond Guarantee Program to serve Native communities most effectively. We have already developed a case study to demonstrate some of the ways that Native CDFIs can participate in the program. This case study was presented at all outreach and training sessions during the FY 2014 round to highlight successful ways the CDFI Bond Guarantee Program can serve Native communities.

In addition, our New Markets Tax Credit Program (NMTC Program) continues to attract new investment capital to Native communities. The purpose of the program is to promote investment in low-income communities by permitting individual and corporate investors to receive a federal tax credit in exchange for making equity investments in specialized financial institutions called Community Development Entities. The NMTC Program is the most competitive program the CDFI Fund administers, and it includes a statutory requirement that non-metropolitan counties receive a proportional allocation of tax credits, helping to ensure that Native communities receive NMTC investment. From 2004 to 2012, NMTC Program investments in Native Communities totaled almost $600 million.

The CDFI Fund's Impact in Native Communities

There is clear evidence that the CDFI Fund's programs promote economic development in Native communities.[2] From 2004 to 2012:

- Native CDFIs that received NACA Program awards made over 15 thousand loans totaling $365 million in Native communities;
- Certified CDFIs that received awards from the CDFI Fund made almost 7,000 loans and investments totaling $184 million in Native communities; and
- Native CDFIs reported that their loans and investments created or retained more than 2,000 jobs.

While these are impressive statistics, we at the CDFI Fund believe that the true impact of our programs cannot be measured by numbers alone, because our work is not just about creating programs and offering services. Our work, and the work of every Native CDFI, is about changing lives and building stronger, more resilient communities.

Here is an example of what I mean.

Four Bands Community Fund, in Eagle Butte, South Dakota, is a Native CDFI that was founded in 2000 to serve the Cheyenne River Sioux Indian Reservation—a territory in rural western South Dakota that is the size of Connecticut and has some of the highest poverty rates in the nation. Four Band Community Fund's programs are based on *Icahya Woecun,* a traditional Lakota model that translates as "the place to grow," and focus on providing loans and training to develop private businesses for the reservation.

Since 2001, Four Bands has received 11 financial assistance and technical assistance awards totaling $4.6 million from the CDFI Fund. From 2000 to 2013, these awards enabled Four Bands to provide 278 credit builder loans and 433 business loans to their community that created or retained 440 jobs. In addition, Four Bands has provided business and financial literacy training to students, prospective entrepreneurs, and other individuals throughout the community.

Among the nearly 5,000 clients that Four Bands has served is Aaron Runs, who used his Credit Builder Loan as a stepping stone to homeownership. As a father of five, Aaron wished to make a permanent home that his children would enjoy, but he knew his credit score was a barrier in reaching that goal. He decided to use the Four Bands Credit Builder Loan to consolidate and pay off multiple debts and was

---

[2] Data includes Native American areas that are federally-designated Native American reservations, Hawaiian homelands, Alaska Native Villages, and U.S. Census Bureau designated Tribal Statistical Areas.

able to increase his credit score by an astounding 90 points in the first year. He now owns a four bedroom home that his children can enjoy.

This is just one of the countless success stories that the CDFI Fund and Native CDFIs are helping to write each year. Together, we are expanding economic opportunity and building stronger and more self-sufficient Native communities.

Conclusion

While we are mindful that these communities still face many challenges, we know that they are resourceful, resilient and capable, because we have seen what can be accomplished. And so we are more committed than ever to serving Native communities and expanding access to capital to those places where access to opportunity is needed most.

On behalf of everyone at Treasury and the CDFI Fund, I would like to express our gratitude to the important work of this Committee, and I look forward to continuing to work with you in the future.

Mr. Chairman, this concludes my formal statement, and I will be happy to answer any of your questions.

The CHAIRMAN. Thank you, Mr. Nolan. Thank you for your statement.

We are going to do things a little bit differently because of the vote. I am going to let Senator Heitkamp go first and I will go last. Then we will swap out depending on who can be chair.

You are up, Senator Heitkamp.

STATEMENT OF HON. HEIDI HEITKAMP, U.S. SENATOR FROM NORTH DAKOTA

Senator HEITKAMP. Thanks so much, and thanks for kind of a rendition of your program.

I just have a couple of quick questions. Some in Indian Country have expressed concern that your bond guarantee program emphasizes land as collateral. We see this all across lending in Indian Country, where land is held in trust or land is allotted and held in trust. There is a lot of concern about that as a policy which really limits the availability of access to a lot of programs, and from what I understand, potentially yours included.

Can you detail the steps Treasury has taken to work with tribes to address the concern?

Mr. NOLAN. Thank you very much for that question, Senator. And also, I would like to take this opportunity to clear up what I think is a common misconception about the bond program, that land is a preferred form of collateral for the program. The program is designed, there are 12 different secondary loan categories. All can be secured by various types of collateral. Land is obviously a choice; it is not the only form of collateral for the program.

I think the type of things we are doing specifically to address the issue that you raised, we are currently looking at the possibility of being able to have what we are calling needs-lease-hold mortgages, which would allow us to be able to accept that as a form of collateral for the program. We have also, as part of our outreach that we just recently conducted in Detroit, San Francisco and in Washington, have developed a case study that is specific to the Native community and how they can better access this program.

So I think we are taking several positive steps to try to improve the access that Native communities have to the program.

Senator HEITKAMP. It is troubling, because securitizing a loan, frequently is it done with land. There is great limitations in terms of number one, even if the tribes wanted to do it, whether it would be advisable.

On a more general level, the nature of collateral in trust lands obviously is a longstanding issue. If you look at kind of your range of products and what you can do, are you looking at developing another line of innovative projects, now that you have this experience working in Indian Country? What would you recommend in terms of additional avenues moving forward to help capitalize business opportunities in Indian Country?

Mr. NOLAN. Senator, in addition to the bond program, which as you know is our newest program, it is the only one of our programs that actually requires collateral, because of the fact that it is a zero subsidy program. Therefore, in order to try and achieve a zero subsidy, we need to be able to have collateral in case of losses in the program to cover those losses. But our other program, the Native CDFI program as well as our CDFI program itself, offers loans and grants which do not require collateral.

Senator HEITKAMP. I guess what I am getting at is, Indian Country, like a lot of other places where you see a higher level of poverty, basically, it lacks financial institutions. That means unless you have a great local community banker in the outlying communities, it becomes very difficult. In fact, we have one Indian Nation in North Dakota that actually has begun a mortgage bank.

So this is not a new problem. It is a problem that I confronted when we ran Housing and Finance in terms of the first-time homeowners program. But I want to also ask you what Treasury has done in collaboration or in discussion with the Department of Interior, in collaboration or discussion with SBA, other kinds of programs, to really build out increased resources and create maybe a broader range of strategies for economic development in Indian Country.

Mr. NOLAN. We have engaged in some discussions, but I get your point and I think we can certainly reach out more to SBA and the other agencies to continue those discussions.

Senator HEITKAMP. And I say this because Senator Dorgan, when he was here, told us about having programs on reservations where one didn't even know what the other was doing and they all had the same mission. So I think it is critically important, as the Secretary has done in Education, bring in all the relevant agencies in this area, for someone to take leadership in economic development, especially capitalizing economic development in Indian Country and bring in all the agencies, streamline the programs, make the programs fit better for the unique situation that we have in Indian Country.

Thank you, Mr. Chairman.

The CHAIRMAN. Senator Begich?

STATEMENT OF HON. MARK BEGICH, U.S. SENATOR FROM ALASKA

Senator BEGICH. Thank you very much, Mr. Chairman, and thank you for being here today.

Mr. Nolan, let me ask, Alaska, as you know, we have the Alaska Community Development Entity, the CDE there that does work. We sent a letter to Treasury about two or three weeks ago. We have had none yet in the last five years, new market tax credit access for any of our entities up in Alaska. In this last round, none came to Alaska.

I know one of the analyses that was done is always like the highest and best benefit and quantity. As you know, a lot of our villages and communities are small and remote. For them, access to capital is even harder, because they are not in an urban area, like the Lower 48, a large urban area where there may be lots of capacity or a lot of history of investment. And I am just wondering, again, we haven't received any new market tax credits since 2009. Which to be frank with you, is very problematic for a State that has half the tribes in the Nation, maybe not by population, but tribes; one-fifth the size by mass of the State and very remote and very tough economic issues in some of our communities.

Can you respond to that? I am a big supporter of the program, I think it is an important program. But when half the tribes in the Nation can't get access to it, that is a problem. Can you give me some thought there?

Mr. NOLAN. Sure. Thank you for the question, Senator.

I would like to start off by saying that the new market tax credit program is really, the CDFI Fund's most oversubscribed program. So for the latest round, we had approximately $25 billion in a request against $3.5 billion in authority. Cumulatively we have over the life of the program approximately $257 billion that has been requested against $40 million in authority. So it is an extremely competitive program.

The second point I would like to make is that it is a very, the competition does not really look at, it is not a place-based program, so it doesn't look at the location of a particular applicant or even with the service area that we serve. But I would like to point out that while I do understand your point that CDFIs in Alaska have not been directly awarded allocations for the past several years, other CDFIs outside of the Alaska area are provided allocations, those that work on a nationwide basis and have a nationwide target market.

So from 2010 to 2012 Alaska did receive $174.6 million in new market tax credit investments. And cumulatively, from the inception of the program, approximately $246 million has been received, with 76 percent of that, however, that has been provided by CDFIs that are outside the State of Alaska. And of that $246 million, approximately $124 million, or 51 percent, has been given to counties within Alaska that are considered non-metropolitan.

So I think even though there has been an issue with the direct allocation to the actual CDEs within Alaska, other CDEs have certainly been making allocations for projects within the State.

Senator BEGICH. Doesn't it then beg the question why don't you just do direct and cut the middleman out? I get what you are saying, that they are national, but somehow once it is allocated out into the nationals, the nationals recognize there is a value. So they are making that happen. Why wouldn't we look at this program and figure out how to make it a little more direct?

Mr. NOLAN. I think because it is the competitive nature of the program, so it is really, as we go through, and again, being oversubscribed, we go through the competitive process and the awards are basically made on a competitive basis. So these other organizations are the ones that have received the allocations; however, they have been able to target Alaska as part of their allocation process.

Senator BEGICH. Let me ask you this and then I will end on this question. Mr. Chairman, thank you for allowing me this.

Obviously your point also is that there are not enough resources for this program that has been beneficial. Is that a fair statement?

Mr. NOLAN. That is a fair statement.

Senator BEGICH. Do you or has the Administration recommended higher amounts that Congress, the Senate, I don't know about the House, because they cut everything. Their investment strategy is no investment. So I get that. Have we reached the levels that you need or are there requests you have made that we have not fulfilled?

Mr. NOLAN. The 2015 President's budget request, we asked for $5 billion for the new market tax credit program as well as a permanent extension of the program.

Senator BEGICH. Right.

Mr. NOLAN. So we have requested increased funding which would allow us then to be able to go further down on the risk of, if we get approximately two times, two to three times the number of applications that we can actually fund. So increased funding would allow us to go farther down on that list.

Senator BEGICH. I am saying this because both Senator Tester and I are on the Appropriations Committee, so I am doing a little opportunity for you. Is the right subcommittee conversation you are having in Appropriations leaving you to believe that on the Senate side, that that amount would be added?

Mr. NOLAN. We don't have any indication at this point where that really is.

Senator BEGICH. That is fair enough. Thank you, Mr. Chairman.

The CHAIRMAN. Thank you, Senator Begich.

First of all, Mr. Nolan, thank you for being here. We appreciate your testimony and appreciate your taking the time.

We will continue with the CDFI conversation. How many total CDFIs are there in this Country?

Mr. NOLAN. Approximately 833.

The CHAIRMAN. How many of that 833 are Native CDFIs?

Mr. NOLAN. We currently have 68.

The CHAIRMAN. Yet over the last two years, it goes to Senator Begich's question, for the last two years, no Native CDFIs were awarded in the program. Now, I know you said it wasn't place-based, and I know you said there are non-Native CDFIs that gave money to Native operations. But why in two years were none of these CDFI's funded that were Native?

Mr. NOLAN. Again, Senator, I think, let me just say that in the last round, 2013, we actually only had two Native CDFIs that actually applied for the program.

The CHAIRMAN. In this very last round?

Mr. NOLAN. In the 2013 round.

The CHAIRMAN. Well, that makes a difference. Okay.

Mr. NOLAN. So we only had two that actually applied. And one of them probably would have made the qualified list to receive an award had we had some further funding. I think it has been partially a low rate of application.

The CHAIRMAN. I got it. So what kind of outreach is done to the Native CDFIs to make sure they know there are programs? I know they are over-subscribed, and they are over-subscribed. And they are a pretty darned good program, too, by the way. So what kind of outreach are you doing to the Native CDFIs to let them know that there is opportunity here, even though it is going to be tough to get that funding, there is still opportunity?

Mr. NOLAN. We have a number of different outreach programs that we have done in the past and some we are planning in the future. Actually, just yesterday we released a request for information to bring a vendor on board who is going to focus on minority CDEs across the board, including Native CDEs. That vendor is specifically going to focus on assisting CDEs with training and other tools to assist them in becoming more successful for the new market tax credit program.

The CHAIRMAN. Okay

Mr. NOLAN. That is actually just something that we just released yesterday.

We have also done, as I mentioned in my opening remarks, the Leadership Journey I and Leadership Journey II as another training series that we have offered for executives and other management of the Native CDFIs to assist them in building organizational capacity, financial funding capacity. So we have offered those as well.

In addition to that, we will be looking at another capacity-building training that we are probably going to start early in the next fiscal year, which will also continue to focus on building capacity in these organizations to be successful in applying and receiving our programs.

The CHAIRMAN. Your testimony has shown that when proper resources are dedicated to Indian Country, good things can happen. Over the last decade, your program and other CDFIs led to $500 million in loans and well over 2,000 jobs. That is significant. Have you seen any trends that would indicate where these programs are more successful in Indian Country?

Mr. NOLAN. Are you talking about locations or programs that are more successful?

The CHAIRMAN. When you are looking at success of the dollars spent, are there any trends that show it is more successful in certain areas or certain tribes than others? And my next question was going to be why. For example, if you have a tribe that is requesting money for maybe a tourism project or an agriculture project or a manufacturing project or an energy project, or whatever else they are working on, is there a pattern to some that are more successful than others? Or is it a mixed bag?

Mr. NOLAN. To be honest, I don't have an immediate answer to that question. But it is certainly something we can look at and I would be happy to get back to you on that.

The CHAIRMAN. It seems like information that might be useful, especially when you are giving the awards out, if you have something that tends to be successful.

The other thing I would also look at is if there are certain tribes that are more successful at it. Then the next question would be, why are they more successful at it. Is it because they have infrastructure the other tribes don't have, or what might it be? If you could take a look at that and get back to us, I think it would be great.

Now, I want to talk about the bond guarantee program. Senator Heitkamp talked about it for a second. You said there are 12 programs, if I heard you correctly.

Mr. NOLAN. Twelve programs.

The CHAIRMAN. One of them requires on land?

Mr. NOLAN. Twelve different loan categories.

The CHAIRMAN. Twelve different loan categories.

Mr. NOLAN. Land is one form of collateral.

The CHAIRMAN. And there are 11 different or other forms of collateral. Talk to me about the bond guarantee program, then, overall. Because with trusted lands, the land thing doesn't work for Indian Country. So what are the other methods of collateral we are talking about, and do any of those methods of collateral fit better with Indian Country than others?

Mr. NOLAN. As I mentioned to Senator Heitkamp, with the land issue, one of the things we are looking at is this idea of being able to take a lease-hold mortgage. And so I think that, and really, we have been working and looking at that, we have been talking to a number of different groups about that. I think that could be a viable alternative to the land issue.

However, we also take other forms of collateral, depending on the type of the loan. It could be equipment, it could be accounts receivable, it could be different forms of collateral, depending on what the actual loan is.

The other thing I wanted to mention in relation to that is, we also have a provision within the program to be able to, what we call principal loss provision, which is basically the possibility of a third party guarantee that takes the place of collateral under the program. So if we can secure from a philanthropic organization or another organization a grant or some other type of collateral, then that can also take the place of collateral. I think that is also something we have been discussing as another potential way to gain entry into the bond program.

The CHAIRMAN. Thank you for that. I think that part of this is going to be an educational process, as you educate the different tribes around the Country.

Tell me this. The position of the CDFI Fund Director was recently vacated. How would you inform an incoming Director on the issues at CDFI affecting Indian Country?

Mr. NOLAN. I think that one of the first things I would discuss is, I think in many cases for us, again, similar to the discussion we were having about the new market tax credit program, the need within Indian Country far exceeds the amount of resources that we have available at the current time to fund those. I think that is definitely something that we will probably want to take up with a new Director.

Then I think also just the bond program is another thing we are certainly looking at. It is a new program. So there has been a lot of growing pains within it, as it relates not only to Indian Country but I think in general that is another program we are going to look at as to how we are able to do additional access with that type of a program.

So I think it is really looking at all of our programs and looking at different ways that we may be able to make changes within the statutes and within the guidelines for these programs, to make them more accessible to Native Americans as well as to others who also find it difficult sometimes to gain entry into these programs.

The CHAIRMAN. Once again, thank you for your testimony. Thank you for what you do. I very much appreciate it. I think if we can get better communication to Indian Country, I think it may help reduce that 50 percent unemployment rate in Indian Country. Thank you very much for being here today, Mr. Nolan.

We are going to have the second panel come up. So Mr. Davis, Mr. Lettig, Mr. Sherman, Mr. Allis and Ms. Rupert, if you could get ready to come up. We will set up our second panel, consisting of a number of organizations that will discuss various perspectives on economic development in Indian Country.

First, we are going to have Gary Davis, President and CEO of the National Center for American Indian Enterprise Development. The National Center has worked for 40 years promoting tribal businesses and individual Indian entrepreneurs. Then we are going to hear from Mike Lettig, who is Executive Vice President of the Native American Financial Services at KeyBank, an institution that has done extensive work in Indian Country and that hopefully dispels the myth that projects in Indian Country are a bad bet.

We will also hear from Gerald Sherman, from Roscoe, Montana, who is Vice Chair of the Native CDFI Network and can tell us how CDFI funds and programs are working on the ground in Indian Country. Good to have you here, Gerald. Then we will turn to Kevin Allis, the Executive Director of the Native American Contractors Association, who is here to discuss Indian business participation in Federal contracting which has been one of the more successful programs across Indian Country. Finally we have Sherry Rupert, President of the Board of Directors of the American Indian Alaska Native Tourism Association, to discuss the growing tourism industry in Indian Country.

Thank you all for being here. Keep your statements to five minutes. Your entire written statement will be a part of the record. With that, I am going to turn the gavel over to Vice Chairman Barrasso, and he can give an opening statement or just hear these guys. I am going to go vote.

STATEMENT OF HON. JOHN BARRASSO, U.S. SENATOR FROM WYOMING

Senator BARRASSO. [Presiding.] Welcome. Go right ahead.

STATEMENT OF GARY DAVIS, PRESIDENT/CEO, NATIONAL CENTER FOR AMERICAN INDIAN ENTERPRISE DEVELOPMENT

Mr. DAVIS. Good afternoon, Senator Tester and members of the Committee dedicated to improve Indian Country. I am Gary Davis, a proud member of the Cherokee Nation of Oklahoma and President and CEO of the National Center for American Indian Enterprise Development. Thank you for inviting us to testify today on Economic Development: Encouraging Investment in Indian Country.

For over 45 years, the National Center has worked to raise the profile of American Indian businesses and to advance economic opportunity for Indian tribes, tribal enterprises and businesses owned by American Indians, Alaska Natives and Native Hawaiians nationwide. I am proud to say that for 22 years, I have enjoyed great success as a Native American entrepreneur, running several private sector businesses. A few years ago, I was asked to join the board of the National Center. After 10 months of serving the organization as a member of its board, I was asked to step up and serve the organization now as its President and CEO.

Since that time, I have become very familiar with the challenges associated with operating a non-profit solely focused on advancing, assisting and developing American Indian businesses and the economy of tribal communities. Those efforts are oftentimes frustrated by Federal programs that provide too few dollars and too many rigid operating and private matching fund requirements in order for them to viable, long-term solutions in helping the National Center accomplish its mission.

This has caused the National Center to reinvest in itself and to develop new programs and initiatives that accomplish its mission and importantly generate financial sustainability for our organization. Subsequently, we serve as an example of the entrepreneurial spirit and self-sufficiency that we encourage to our American Indian enterprises and entrepreneurs.

The National Center is the Nation's leading and longest-serving advocate and provider of American Indian business development assistance. Every day, we encourage investment in Indian Country by assisting and promoting Native business interests and commercial and government marketplaces, both domestic and international.

For nearly 30 years, we have also produced reservation economic summits, known by the acronym RES. Our RES events also help us generate the revenues we need to meet our Federal program requirements and enhance our operations. Our RES events include business development and training sessions, forums, trade shows and procurement and business matchmaking expos to encourage corporations and Federal agencies to buy from American Indian suppliers.

As we speak, this hearing is being streamed into our first Reservation Economic Summit in D.C. for hundreds of our conference participants to see and hear this important proceeding. This week's three-day RES D.C. Summit being held at the Omni Shoreham Hotel here in the Nation's capital covers many topics, including the Buy Indian Act, global trade, CDFIs, Native ANA contracting, energy, telecommunications, technology, e-commerce and much more.

The National Center serves as a facilitator, a connector and closer to ensure investment in Indian Country. We are now gearing up to expand trade opportunities for tribes, tribal enterprises and all Native-owned businesses through our Native American Global Trade Center, which is funded by the United Parcel Service, UPS. We are sustaining economic momentum by holding our Reservation

Economic Summits every four months across Indian Country on tribal lands to serve as economic launch pads for Indian Country's enterprises and our corporate partners. Beginning this September, we will offer internet-based business development and training through our National Center Edge web portal.

The National Center is progressing because of lessons learned. Here are some of those lessons. First, the hand up works better than the handout approach to instill self-determination and self-sufficiency. Second, Federal business development programs are more successful if they are designed specifically to help startups and larger companies in Indian Country and include consultation from organizations like the National Center who work for Indian business each day and know their needs.

Third, adequate Federal funding, whether through direct appropriations or contracts, really does help technical assistance organizations improve their performance and enables them to scale up and attract better educated, better experienced trainers and business counselors to serve their Indian Country clients.

Fourth, Federal responsiveness improves with a high level Native American or tribal liaison office with its own staff and budget. These offices now exist in nearly every economic focused Federal entity: HUD, USDA, Energy, Treasury, FCC and SBA. It is past time for the Department of Commerce to beef up its office focused on Indian Country. At least two specific laws enacted in 2000 direct Commerce to advance business and economic development, trade and tourism promotion in Indian Country, P.L. 106–447 and P.L. 106–464. The current senior advisor on Native American affairs now must devote half his time to his intergovernmental affairs office duties. However, if the Native American office had its own budget, it could do more than advance the President's initiatives, it could start fulfilling the directives enacted 14 years ago.

The National Center thanks Senator Mark Begich for pursuing a Senate Floor amendment to the fiscal year 2015 Commerce appropriations in order to make existing funds available to provide for this office of Commerce its own budget. At least 12 national and regional Native organizations have endorsed such a move.

Sixth, Indian Country programs that work should be reinforced. Good examples are two programs the National Center has supported since endorsing them in 1987 and 1990 testimony before the Senate Indian Affairs leadership. One, the Buy Indian Act and two, the Indian Loan Guarantee Program.

To wrap up, the National Center calls for the following executive and congressional actions, which I recommended two months ago on April 30th to the Senate leadership and is outlined at the end of my written testimony. The National Center applauds the Committee for reporting to the full Senate Chairman Tester's bill, S. 2188, a Carcieri fix, and Ranking Member Barrasso's Tribal Energy Development Bill, S. 2132. Now Congress must pass these and others to help tribes and businesses in Indian Country overcome judicial, regulatory and financial barriers.

We ask the Committee to hold three additional oversight hearings, one on Buy Indian Act enforcement, one on expanding the Native American Affairs Office at the Department of Commerce, and one on e-commerce, including legitimate and compliant online lending by tribes who are dependent on the internet for revenue generation.

For our part, we will continue to work tirelessly to help attract the business partners and investors, whether tribal, national or even international, to fulfill our mission as the National Center for American Indian Enterprise Development. Thank you again for inviting the National Center's testimony today.

[The prepared statement of Mr. Davis follows:]

PREPARED STATEMENT OF GARY DAVIS, PRESIDENT/CEO, NATIONAL CENTER FOR AMERICAN INDIAN ENTERPRISE DEVELOPMENT

Good afternoon, Chairman Tester and members of this extraordinary Senate Committee dedicated to improving Indian Country. I am Gary Davis, President and CEO of the National Center for American Indian Enterprise Development. I thank the Committee for inviting the National Center to testify today on "Economic Development: Encouraging Investment in Indian Country." The National Center embraces that challenge every day in serving nationwide with thousands of Indian tribes, tribal enterprises, and businesses owned by American Indians, Alaska Natives and Native Hawaiians.

The National Center, now in its 5th decade, is the Nation's leading and longest serving advocate and provider of American Indian business development assistance. Every day, the National Center works in the private sector and collaborates with private and public sector players to encourage investment in Indian Country by assisting and promoting Native business interests in commercial and government marketplaces, both domestic and international. We also produce national and regional Reservation Economic Summits (RES) and Trade Shows. As we speak, this hearing is being streamed into the National Center's first RES DC for hundreds of our conference participants to hear and see this important proceeding.

This week's DC Summit, Trade Show and Buy Native Matchmaking Expo runs June 24–26 at the Omni Shoreham Hotel, with workshops and trainings on a broad range of topics, including:

- Buy Indian Act regulations and enforcement
- International export and trade investment initiatives
- Native Community Development Financial Institutions and CDFI bond guarantees
- The state of Native 8(a) contracting
- Energy and economic development initiatives and investment opportunities
- Telecommunication solutions facilitated by tribes, the FCC, USDA, and Congress
- Technology innovations to power E-commerce, encourage investment, and spur job creation and business growth in Indian Country.

The National Center's Role in Encouraging Investment in Indian Country

Our non-profit organization launched in 1969 to assist individual American Indian-owned businesses in building their businesses by connecting them with larger, well-established companies as business partners and mentors. Many of these larger companies—in the energy, technology and defense sectors—became National Center partners by serving on our National Resource Council.

As the Federal Government began to step up its entrepreneurial development, business and procurement technical assistance efforts, the National Center became one of the first American Indian organizations to advocate and partner with some of the federal agencies. One of our founders, David Lester, served on the advisory group that conceived of what President Nixon then launched in his 1971 Executive Order as the Minority Business Development Agency (MBDA). The National Center developed and operated the first of what became a group of Native American Business Development Centers. (In 2012, MBDA converted them all to Minority Business Centers.) The National Center also worked with Congress to expand the Defense Logistics Agency's Procurement Technical Assistance Program to create American Indian Procurement Technical Assistance Centers (AIPTACs) in the 1980s. The National Center launched and still operates the longest serving and most successful AIPTAC. We collaborate with the Montana and other four AIPTACs whose clients benefit from our RES conferences that always include trade shows and extraordinary procurement matchmaking expos.

The National Center leaders also have long advocated for broader use of Buy Indian Act authority. In 1987 and 1990 testimony before the Senate Indian Affairs leadership, then President Steve Stallings urged strengthening Buy Indian Act provisions to apply beyond the Bureau of Indian Affairs (BIA) and Indian Health Service (IHS) to other federal agencies that expend funds for the benefit of American Indians and Alaska Natives. It took 20 more years, over 100 altogether, for BIA to propose implementing regulations in 2010. As the National Center wrote in its May, 2010 comments on BIA's proposed rule, energizing and strengthening Indian enterprises through robust government contracting set asides is a tool that BIA, Interior and other departments should continue to develop to invigorate tribal and Indian enterprise growth. To be as expansive and inclusive as possible, the National Center urged that the final regulations: (1) be made applicable to every Bureau or Office that has delegated authority to complete acquisitions under the Buy Indian Act; (2) outline the overall goal of 100 percent utilization of Indian economic enterprises; (3) provide for an Accountability Officer responsible for monitoring compliance and reporting annually to the Secretary on the extent of use and amount of contracts awarded to Indian economic enterprises. The final regulations published in July, 2013 reflected many of the National Center's comments, but unfortunately did not include the recommended goal of 100 percent utilization of Native enterprises.

Today, many federal departments and agencies expend funds for the benefit of Indians but do not utilize procedures designed to ensure that such "benefit" is extended through contracting, purchasing and hiring policies or activities. That is a shame, because expanded Buy Indian Act authority could encourage investment in Indian Country, create jobs and strengthen tribal economies in its requirements for maximum employment of Indian labor and purchase of Indian goods and services.

Two other recommendations made at the 1987 Senate hearing referenced above—which Congress took quick action to pass—were amendments to the Indian Finance Act to encourage more business and economic development activity in Indian Country by tribes, tribal enterprises and companies owned by individual American Indians and Alaska Natives by:

1. allowing prime contractors 5 percent incentive payments for awarding some of their federal contract dollars to Indian-owned economic enterprises (incentive payments worth 5 percent of the value of the subcontract work performed by the Indian subcontractor); and
2. increasing to $500 million the total amount of loans eligible under the Indian Loan Guarantee Program. In 2006, Congress raised the level even higher to $1.5 billion.

Sadly, none of the federal agencies did anything to implement the 5 percent Indian Incentive Program (IIP) authority. So, tribal-owned contractors urged Congress to help intercede with the Department of Defense (DOD), by far the largest federal contracting agency. Congress did so by including provisions in the Defense Appropriations FY 1990 to fund IIP payments. As DOD took no implementing action in that year, the next fiscal year's DOD appropriations measure directed promulgation of implementing regulations within 90 days. Finally after DOD streamlined its regulations and inserted specific IIP clauses in DOD contracts, the IIP became successful in helping to generate well over $300 million annually in subcontract dollars to Native-owned companies. In recent years, backlogs of DOD-approved IIP requests have always exceeded the annual appropriation of $15 million for the payments, evidencing the program's success in enabling Native businesses to market their capabilities and land contract work. For many tribes, the IIP has been key to incentivizing DOD contractors to subcontract work to tribal enterprises which, in turn, have expanded their operations to help build their tribal economies.

As to the Indian Loan Guarantee Program, however, Congress has never appropriated the full amounts authorized, and has so short-changed the credit subsidy for this essential program that BIA has not been able to guarantee loans totaling more than about $300 million per year.

Today, the National Center sees its mission as not only to encourage and advocate for American Indian Enterprise Development, but also to serve as a facilitator, a connector, and closer to ensure investment in Indian Country. We serve tribal communities and tribal enterprises, companies owned by tribal members and shareholders, and all the private and public entities interested in partnering with these Native businesses. We link investors, lenders, guarantors, co-producers, purchasers, suppliers, joint venture mentors and protégés—whether the relationships are intra-tribal, inter-tribal, national or international.

As The National Center for American Indian Enterprise Development, we want to lead the charge in opening up trade and export opportunities for tribes, tribal enterprises and all Native-owned businesses. We are accomplishing this push with our

National and Regional Reservation Economic Summits as economic development launch pads for these Indian Country enterprises and our corporate partners. We also will offer web-based business development through our National Center Edge portal, proactively utilizing technology and the Internet to provide economic opportunities, trainings, business development services, and much more, to tribes and Native businesses nationwide. The National Center's Native American Global Trade Center will expand to introduce and facilitate more global opportunities and relationships for tribes and tribal enterprises. As the world becomes smaller through technology and the Internet, the National Center is strategically positioning to facilitate both domestic and international trade for Indian Country.

Just as other nonprofits and businesses must operate today, the National Center must be lean, mean, efficient and effective. Working out of small offices, strategically located, perhaps even in Washington, DC, we will continue to collaborate with corporate and tribal partners to maximize synergies and reduce operational costs. As a national organization, we will continue building key relationships in DC and working partnerships with federal agencies and Congress to improve business and economic program delivery to, and increase investment in, Indian Country.

Lessons Learned

The National Center first welcomed me as private sector entrepreneur running several successful businesses. After joining the National Center's Board of Directors and now as President and CEO, I am grasping the challenge of running a nonprofit serving businesses and tribal communities with funds from a mix of federal cooperative assistance agreements with rigid operating constraints, and private sector funds to supplement, sustain, and enhance our operations. Creativity and inspiration in our RES conferences, trade shows and other trainings help generate the revenues we need to sustain and grow. Below are some of our lessons learned:

First, some federal programs have been more helpful than others for Indian Country. The "hand up" works better than the "hand out" approach to instill self-determination and self-sufficiency.

Second, based on the National Center's direct experience, the more successful federal business development programs are those that are specifically designed to help startups and larger companies in Indian Country. What does not work well is the "square peg—round hole" approach of repackaging legacy federal programs and dictating how assistance must be delivered and to what size of business. Least successful are those programs that focus on getting the highest possible return on the federal investment by requiring business assistance centers to work only with American Indian businesses generating well over $1 million in annual revenues—not the Indian business startups that most need the entrepreneurial development assistance. The Small Business Administration (SBA) recently took the right approach in announcing a PRIME grant program that calls for proposals from tribes and other entities willing to serve micro enterprises.

Third, adequate federal funding has been key to the more successful Indian Country-focused programs that provide technical assistance to users of the federal programs. Whether through direct appropriations (e.g., National American Indian Housing Council) or contracts to provide the technical assistance (e.g., Oweesta Corporation), stronger federal support enables technical assistance organizations to scale up and attract better educated and experienced trainers and business counselors.

Fourth, another key has been establishment of a high level Office of Native American Affairs or Tribal Liaison within the major federal departments and agencies operating programs that can advance business and economic development in Indian Country. For years, the Department of the Interior's BIA and IHS paid primary attention to Indian Country's needs. Broader federal attention started to occur when the Department of Housing and Urban Development formed the Office of Native American Programs, and then Congress passed the Native American Housing and Self Determination Act. The SBA started to improve its assistance to American Indian- and tribal-owned businesses and contractors with establishment of its Office of Native American Affairs with increased funding. The Federal Communications Commission (FCC) became more responsive to Indian Country needs with establishment of its Office of Native American Affairs and Policy. The Department of Agriculture (USDA) expanded its outreach and improved program delivery to Indian Country with establishment of the Office of Tribal Liaison. Congress saw the wisdom of that approach and codified the Office with line item funding in the Farm Bill enactment. Likewise, the Congress embraced and funded the Department of Energy's Office of Indian Energy Policy and Programs.

Fifth, a major push is needed to fulfill Congress' intent for the Department of Commerce to pay far greater attention to its mandates to advance business and economic development, trade and tourism promotion in Indian Country. Back in the late 1990s, then Commerce Secretary William Daley took administrative action to establish an office for Native American Affairs reporting directly to the Secretary. Congress recognized the importance of Commerce's portfolio to advancement of Indian Country's interests and passed two important measures that became law in 2000:

- The Indian Tribal Regulatory Reform and Business Development Act (Public Law 106–447) directed the Secretary of Commerce, in consultation with the Secretary of the Interior and others, to establish a Regulatory Reform and Business Development on Indian Lands Authority to facilitate identification and subsequent removal of obstacles to investment, business development, and creation of wealth for the economies of Native American communities. The Authority was allotted one year to do its work and report back to Congress, and disband within 3 months thereafter.

- The Native American Business Development, Trade Promotion and Tourism Act (Public Law 106–464) codified an Office of Native American Business Development headed by a Director, appointed by and reporting to the Secretary, to fulfill enumerated duties of the Secretary, including to: (1) ensure intra- and inter-agency coordination of federal programs that provide financial and technical assistance for business and economic development, and expansion of trade; (2) carry out a Native American export and trade promotion program; (3) conduct a Native American tourism program; and (4) report annually to the Senate Committee on Indian Affairs and House Committee on Natural Resources on the operation of the Office and any recommendations for legislation that the Secretary, in consultation with the Office's Director, deems necessary to carry out the Secretary's duties under the Act.

Recently, Washington Congresswoman Del Bene introduced the "Indian Country Economic Revitalization Act of 2014" (H.R. 4699) to amend the second of these two Acts to require the Secretary to prepare and submit to the House Committee on Natural Resources and Senate Committee on Indian Affairs, a report and recommendations for promoting the sustained growth of the economies of Indian tribes and Indian lands. Such a report would be due within one year of the bill's enactment and each year thereafter for 3 years.

Here's the big problem. Unfortunately, no action was ever taken to establish the Authority mandated in Public Law 106–447, and only minimal steps have been taken since 2000 to implement Public Law 106–464. In 2005, the MBDA Director agreed to become Director of the Office of Native American Business Development and allocate about $200,000 to hire an experienced Native American to develop a business plan and begin fulfilling the requirements of the two Acts above. Three Native Americans, successively, have since held that position, with the latter two also designated at the Senior Advisor to the Secretary on Native American Affairs. The current Senior Advisor is now housed in the Inter-Governmental Affairs Office and doing his best to help implement President Obama's new Indian Country initiatives. However, with its own budget for more than just one person, the Office of Native American Business Development could help implement the President's new initiatives, and fulfill the Secretary's duties under the two Acts (and possibly others).

The National Center wishes to thank Alaska Senator Mark Begich for offering to pursue a Senate floor amendment to the FY 2015 Commerce Appropriations measure to make available, within the existing Departmental Management budget, specific funds to provide the Office its own budget. Twelve national and regional Native organizations are on record supporting such a move, and we all will work to secure this funding at long last.

The National Center calls on this Committee and the entire Congress to step up and provide the targeted funding and impetus to improve the programs that enable tribes and Native businesses to succeed on their own terms. In recent years, the National Center has taken the lead to develop, in coordination with other national Native organizations, the key recommendations and specific funding requests for the federal programs that leverage non-federal dollars to catalyze economic growth in Indian Country. Just two months ago on April 30, the National Center presented these specific recommendations to the Senate leadership and they are listed at the end of my testimony.

National Center Recommendations for Executive and Congressional Action

Review the Buy Indian Act for Enforcement and Impact

During his recent visit to the Standing Rock Sioux Community, President Obama announced a new Interior initiative to improve Buy Indian Act implementation and increase Interior procurement purchases by 10 percent. That is a step in the right direction. To hear how BIA and IHS are progressing in their use of Buy Indian Act procedures in their procurement awards and purchases, the National Center hosted a RES DC workshop yesterday to receive their progress reports. Within the coming months, we urge this Committee to conduct an oversight hearing to receive testimony and reports from these and other agencies with update on their use of Buy Indian Act authority. The Committee also should seek testimony on how to expand the Act's application to additional federal departments and agencies.

Ensure Expansion of Commerce's Office Devoted to Native American Affairs

For years, the National Center and other national Native organizations have urged expansion of this Office reporting directly to the Secretary of Commerce and line item funding for this Office within Commerce's Departmental Management budget. This key Office must fulfill the duties prescribed in Public Laws 106–447 and 464 to implement Indian policy initiatives and expand Native American business development, trade promotion and tourism initiatives both domestically and internationally in collaboration with other agencies within Commerce and other cabinet departments and agencies. The National Center is raising this issue in the RES DC panel discussion on international trade. President Obama's recently announced initiatives to support growth of new markets and improve access to export opportunities can be accelerated if Commerce provides funding for a more robust Office of Native American Affairs. In addition, we urge this Committee to do its part by pressing for expansion and funding for this important Office.

Erase Discrimination and Restore Parity Disrupted by the ''Carcieri'' Decision

For Indian Country to be able to attract investment, create jobs and build tribal economies, all federally recognized Indian tribes must be able to protect and enhance their tribal lands, and generate self-sustaining income from tribal lands. The Interior Department decisions and opinions have gone as far as they can to restore parity among tribes striving to reacquire some of their original land base. Congress must take long overdue action to pass legislation to clarify the authority of the Interior Secretary to acquire land in trust for any federally recognized tribe so as to remedy confusion and harmful impacts stemming from the U.S. Supreme Court's decision in *Carcieri v. Salazar*. That decision has caused processing delays in trust land applications, additional bureaucratic red tape for potential investors, and confusion over legal jurisdiction. The National Center applauds this Committee for reporting the needed remedial legislation to the full Senate on June 12 for further action.

Promote Tax Parity for Tribes

The National Center commends enactment of authority for Indian tribes to issue tax exempt Tribal Economic Development (TED) Bonds, and the Obama Administrative iterative implementation to encourage tribes to use TED bonds to finance economic development projects, such as laying new broadband fiber, improving access to clean water, building hotels for tourists and manufacturing plants. With the TED Bond provisions, Congress took an important step toward providing more parity in the tax treatment of tribal, state and municipal governments. Likewise, in action on tax reform or any other tax legislation, it must be ensured that tribal governments are treated as taxing authorities in any provisions for collecting remote sales taxes (in parity with state and local governments and other taxing authorities). As sovereigns, tribes must be able to exercise the right to collect tax revenues to provide for their members and promote business and job creation, and even offer tax advantages to attract outside investment necessary to build their tribal economies.

Support More Measures to Encourage Energy Investment and Development

In numerous energy-related workshops hosted at our National RES and RES DC conferences, there has been great interest in development of renewable and conventional energy resources, and the related potential for workforce and economic development. President Obama fully recognizes this interest and recently announced new initiatives to remove regulatory barriers to energy and infrastructure development on Indian land by streamlining approval processes for rights-of-way, including transition lines and broadband access. Congress also must act by passing legislation that provides tribes options and funding mechanisms to develop their energy resources, respects tribes' ability to regulate the development of their own resources, and removes unnecessary regulatory barriers to American Indian energy development.

Enact FY 2015 Funding that Spurs Business and Economic Development in Indian Country

The most obvious action that Congress can take is appropriating adequate funding for programs that improve access to tools for tribes and their members to make freer and better use of their lands, grow businesses, create more jobs, access more income streams, improve their infrastructure (roads, utilities, housing, schools, community centers, health clinics, government operations, courts) and pursue larger scale business and resource development. Below are the National Center's specific requests for FY 2015 funding actions:

Department of the Interior

• $25 million for the Office of Indian Energy and Economic Development (OIEED)

OIEED should receive more funding and latitude to: (1) speed the HEARTH Act's implementation; (2) develop a model tribal environmental code that tribes could consider, adapt and implement along with new tribal ordinances for leasing tribal lands for energy and economic development projects; (3) provide funding to requesting tribes for business plans or feasibility studies for business and economic development projects; (4) expand the scope and usefulness of its Indian Loan Guarantee Program to finance more business operations and expansions, provide standby letters of credit that could encourage sureties to provide needed surety bonding, and finance start up energy and economic development projects; and (5) provide more technical assistance (including providing guidance on preparing business plans, repairing credit records, and completing loan applications).

• $15 million for the Indian Loan Guarantee Program

OIEED's Division of Capital Investment oversees the Indian Loan Guarantee Program and loan subsidy program, and has authority to support surety bonding for American Indian contractors. The Loan Guarantee Program is the only federal guarantee program that facilitates the process for eligible tribal and individual American Indian borrowers to obtain conventional lender financing for businesses and economic development projects. BIA-certified lenders are willing and able to lend to Tribes and Indian businesses on reservations and submit to tribal court jurisdiction (whereas SBA-certified lenders must adjudicate loan defaults in federal court). OIEED also operates a revolving credit facility (SBA has no such support) that assists American Indian borrowers with lines of credit for working capital, payrolls for hiring new employees, and even assurances sufficient for sureties to provide performance bonds to tribal- and other Native-owned contractors. As noted earlier in this testimony, Congress authorized a substantial increase in the aggregate limit on Indian loan and surety bond guarantees from $500 million to $1.5 billion in 2006. Congress has so far failed to approve a parallel hike in the credit subsidy, but it can start by providing at least $15 million for FY 2015 to permit guarantee of total loan principal up to about $240 million.

Department of Commerce

• At least $1 million for Commerce's Office of Native American Affairs

This line item funding is essential to expand the Office of Native American Affairs (ONAA) contemplated in the Native American Business Development, Trade Promotion and Tourism Act of 2000. Line item ONAA funding within Commerce's Departmental Management budget will better enable the Office to implement Indian policy initiatives and expand Native American business development, trade promotion and tourism initiatives both domestically and internationally in collaboration with other agencies within Commerce and other cabinet departments and agencies. Line item funding for the ONAA is particularly important since Commerce's Minority Business Development Agency has eliminated the Native American-focused business enterprise centers that provided valuable business assistance for many years to tribes, tribal enterprises and individual Native-owned businesses and Native entrepreneurs.

Small Business Administration

• At least $1.25 million for SBA's Office of Native American Affairs

The SBA Office of Native American Affairs (ONAA) plays an integral role in helping tribes and Native businesses access SBA's many business assistance and lending programs. Fortunately the line item for ''Native American Outreach'' funding has increased somewhat, but a specific budget for the ONAA would better enable the Office to expand its successful activities that: (1) spur business development with SBA loans, loan guarantees and surety bond guarantees; (2) provide tribal and business executive training; and (3) engage in multi-agency workshops and native supplier initiative events around the U.S., as recently announced by President Obama during his visit to Standing Rock. At that time, Standing Rock announced approval of its Tribal Uniform Commercial Code. This news was welcome, and a tribute to groundwork supported in part by SBA and the Federal Reserve Board of Minneapolis to assist Indian tribes in considering and adopting business ordinances modeled on the UCC. It is especially important to fund the ONAA adequately given the loss of funding for the Small Business Teaming Grant program that supported two centers focused on teaming among tribal and other Native-owned contractors.

Federal Communications Commission

- $2 million for the FCC's Office of Native Affairs and Policy

The FCC–ONAP jump-started an expansive educational effort within the agency and in Indian Country on telecommunications issues and programs. ONAP promotes increased Internet, broadband and telecommunications access for tribal communities that suffer from the lowest penetration rates for basic telephone service and broadband. Today's economy relies heavily on E-commerce for business growth and job creation. The ONAP helps ensure that FCC and other federal decisions properly address Indian Country's needs for better electronic communication.

Department of Agriculture

- $1.5 million for USDA's Office of Tribal Relations

The OTR reports directly to the USA Secretary and serves a linchpin role in expanding all USDA program support throughout Indian Country. Congress should appropriate adequate funding for OTR and USDA-Rural Development programs that support economic development activities in Indian Country by providing loans, loan guarantees, grants and other assistance for business and economic development, telecommunications, water systems and other infrastructure deployment, international trade in agricultural products, and crop insurance.

Department of Defense

- $4.5 million for AIPTACs within $36,262 million for Procurement Technical Assistance

Since 1990, the Defense Logistics Agency (DLA) has supported Procurement Technical Assistance through cooperative agreements with regional, statewide and local centers (PTACs), and American Indian PTACs that serve at least two BIA Areas. Six such AIPTACs now exist across the U.S., and all PTACs must raise private funds to make the match that DLA requires and to sustain operations. AIPTACs offer valuable assistance to tribal and other Native-owned companies in navigating the large, complex federal procurement market, winning government contracts and complying with myriad government procurement and other regulatory requirements. Last year, Congress increased the authorization levels for statewide PTACs and AIPTACs. In turn, Congress should increase the amount reserved for AIPTACs ($4.5 million) within at least level funding of $36,262 million for the overall program.

- $15 million for the 5 percent Indian Incentive Payment Program

Section 504 of the Indian Finance Act authorized, and DOD regulations implemented, the 5 percent Indian Incentive Payment (IIP) Program that permits a DOD higher tier contractor to receive an IIP of 5 percent of the value of a subcontract it awards to a Native-owned subcontractor or supplier. DOD's Office of Small Business Programs reviews such requests which, if approved, are paid from funds appropriated for the IIP. Since FY 1991, Congress annually has appropriated funds for DOD to make these 5 percent IIP payments. As noted earlier in this testimony, the IIP program has helped generate well over $300 million annually in subcontract dollars to Native-owned companies in recent years. The backlog of IIP requests always exceeds the amount appropriated for the payments, evidencing the program's success in enabling Native businesses to market their capabilities and land contract work. For many tribes, the IIP has been key to incentivizing DOD contractors to subcontract work to tribal enterprises which, in turn, have expanded their operations to help build their tribal economies.

Department of Treasury

- $15 million for Native Community Development Financial Institutions

Indian Country has benefitted significantly from the Native Initiative of the Community Development Financial Institutions Fund (CDFI Fund) through expanded access to capital for individuals and small businesses. The initiative funds Native CDFIs to provide micro loans and facilitates financial literacy and entrepreneurial development training in Native communities across the country.

Once again, thank you, Mr. Chairman, and the Committee for the opportunity to present testimony on behalf of the National Center and our recommendations. We urge the Senate, and House, to consider and act on these matters promptly.

Senator BARRASSO. Thank you very much, Mr. Davis, for your testimony. We appreciate your being here and joining the Committee today.

Mr. Lettig, welcome to you and we will appreciate hearing what you have to say. Thank you.

STATEMENT OF WILLIAM "MIKE" LETTIG, EXECUTIVE VICE PRESIDENT, NATIONAL EXECUTIVE NATIVE AMERICAN FINANCIAL SERVICES AND AGRIBUSINESS, KEYBANK

Mr. LETTIG. Thank you, Vice Chairman Barrasso and members of the Committee. Thank you for inviting me today and giving me the opportunity to testify on the role investment can play in encouraging economic development in Indian Country. My name is Mike Lettig and I lead the KeyBank's Native American Financial Services segment, which is part of our community bank.

KeyBank is a regional bank headquartered in Cleveland, Ohio, with approximately $93 billion in assets. Our customer base spans retail, small business and corporate investment clients. We have over 14,000 employees and approximately 1,000 branches spread across 12 States in our footprint.

KeyBank has provided financial solutions to Indian Country for more than 50 years. Over the past five years, KeyBank has helped raise more than $3 billion in capital for Indian Country and we are on track in assisting and raise more than a billion dollars this year alone. We at KeyBank consider this to be very important work.

As President Obama noted during his visit to Indian Country, there are still wide disparities, both among tribes and Native Americans in general, and the U.S. population as a whole. While Native Americans living on reservations have seen personal income nearly double in real terms since 1970 the average poverty rates for these communities from 2006 through 2010 was 30 percent compared with 14 percent nationally. Child poverty rate was more than 15 percent higher than the national average of 36 percent.

We are grateful for the opportunity to help bridge these disparities by assisting Indian Country leadership in raising capital and by doing so, gaining confidence in their ability to set good fiscal policy and practice. I am very pleased to be here today to share my perspective on how the private sector investments can help foster significant economic development in Indian Country. Based on my years of experience working with Indian Country leaders, I have developed a little bit of an understanding of the challenges, real and perceived, that hamper the timely investment in infrastructure in Indian Country and as a result, delays much-needed economic development.

Despite notable progress over recent years, there still remains private sector uncertainty about whether Indian Country is a good investment. This uncertainty, which I believe is based on lack of information and understanding about Indian Country, has a chilling effect on the capital market's appetite for investing in Native America. Most of these challenges, such as the lack of experience in dealing with Native sovereigns, are well known and I won't deal with those today.

Economic development is also stymied by regulatory barriers to infrastructure development. For example, all new infrastructure construction on tribal lands require rights-of-way approval. It is a time-consuming and cumbersome process and I applaud and look forward to seeing the Bureau of Indian Affairs' formal proposal to streamline this process.

I also applaud the plans for training to help tribal leaders implement the HEARTH Act and in so doing, empower tribes to establish and enforce land leasing regulations rather than relying on the BIA for approval.

Indian Country faces continued challenges in developing a workforce that is prepared to meet these business needs. As the President noted, Native American students continue to lag behind their peers on national assessments and lead in the highest dropout rates for any racial or ethnic population, and hold a dramatically lower share of the baccalaureate degrees that the rest of the population has.

While we need to raise the bar for all learners in the United States to ensure that our future workforce can compete in a global economy, Indian Country students have higher hurdles than most in order to compete.

Challenges specific to doing business in Indian Country exist, but it is clear the tribes continue to take steps in developing their economics. For example, many tribes such as the Navajo Nation, the Muskogee Creek Nation, Puyallup Tribe, Shoshone Bannock have developed sophisticated judicial and legal systems. Tribes continue to develop disciplined, strategic plans. Developing infrastructure, whether that involves roads, schools or utilities, are a high priority. Strong infrastructure is essential to tribal members' quality of life as well as economic development.

Tribal human capital is improving. There are increasing numbers of Native Americans in law, medicine and finance who are contributing to their communities. And there is continued focus on developing stronger working relationships with multiple jurisdictional interests, such as cities, counties, States and the Federal entities.

Tribes and the private sector must develop mutually acceptable terms on several issues in order to attract capital. Some tribes and the private sector need clear and enforceable business agreements. Tribes and the private sector must develop dispute resolution processes. This entails tribes and the private sector developing mutually acceptable agreements on the sovereign immunity issue and choice of law.

Still, there are a number of obstacles. By transferring authority to tribes and streamlining the review process, as is proposed in the recommended enhancements to the Indian Tribal Energy Development and Self-Determination Act Amendment of 2014, the government can help Indian Country more easily attract interest in energy development. Government needs to continue to identify simple and accountable ways to reduce Federal review or approval and continue a responsible transfer of authority to Indian leadership. Government can continue to facilitate economic development by supporting the existing incentives, such as new market tax credits, low income housing tax credits and tribal economic development bonds.

I want to note that KeyBank believes in helping all our communities, including our Indian Country communities. Reducing the review process and creating more autonomy for tribes to attract investments by the private sector will enhance the ability of Indian Country leaders to help their own communities thrive. With experience in Indian Country by the private sector, they will come to understand that Indian Country is a dynamic place to do business, that mutually acceptable tools can be developed and build Indian Country economic independence and sustained quality of life for Native America.

[The prepared statement of Mr. Lettig follows:]

PREPARED STATEMENT OF WILLIAM "MIKE" LETTIG, EXECUTIVE VICE PRESIDENT, NATIONAL EXECUTIVE NATIVE AMERICAN FINANCIAL SERVICES AND AGRIBUSINESS, KEYBANK

Introduction

Chairman Tester, Vice Chairman Barasso, and Members of the Committee, thank you for inviting me to today's hearing and giving me the opportunity to testify on the role investment can play in encouraging economic development in Indian Country.

My name is Mike Lettig, and I lead KeyBank's Native American Financial Services segment, which is part of our KeyBank Community Bank.

KeyBank is a regional bank headquartered in Cleveland with approximately $93 billion in assets. KeyCorp's customer base spans retail, small business, corporate, and investment clients. KeyCorp has more than 14,000 employees, and approximately 1,000 KeyBank branches spread across 12 states within in our retail branch footprint.

KeyBank has provided financial solutions to Indian Country for more than 50 years. Over the past five years, KeyBank has helped to raise more than $3 billion in capital for Indian Country, and we are on track to assist in raising more than $1 billion this year alone.

We at KeyBank consider this to be very important work. As President Obama noted during his recent historic visit to Indian Country, there are still wide disparities both among tribes and Native Americans in general and the U.S. population as a whole. While Native Americans living on reservations have seen personal income nearly double in real terms since 1970, the average poverty rate for these communities from 2006–2010 was 30 percent, compared with 14 percent nationally, and the child poverty rate was more than 15 percent higher than the national average of 36 percent.

We are grateful for the opportunity to help bridge these disparities by assisting Indian Country leadership in raising capital and, by doing so, gaining confidence in their ability to set good fiscal policy and practice.

I am very pleased to be here today to share my perspective on how private sector investment can foster significant economic development in Indian Country.

Based on my years of experience working with Indian Country leaders, I have developed an understanding of challenges—real and perceived—that hamper the timely investment into infrastructures in Indian Country and as a result delay much-needed economic development.

Despite notable progress over recent years, there still remains private sector uncertainty about whether Indian Country is a good investment. This uncertainty—which I believe is based on lack of information and understanding about Indian Country—has a chilling effect on capital markets' appetite for investing in Native America.

Most of these challenges, such as lack of experience in dealing with Native sovereigns, are well known, and I won't detail them here.

Economic development is stymied by regulatory barriers to infrastructure development. For example, all new infrastructure construction on tribal lands requires "rights-of-way" approval. This is a time-consuming and cumbersome process. I applaud and look forward to seeing the Bureau of Indian Affair's s formal proposal to streamline this process. In the same spirit, I applaud plans for training to help tribal leaders implement the HEARTH Act and in so doing to empower tribes to establish and enforce land leasing regulations rather than relying on BIA lease approval.

Indian Country faces continuing challenges in developing a workforce that is prepared to meet business needs. As President Obama also noted, Native American students continue to lag behind their peers on national assessments, to account for the highest dropout rate of any racial or ethnic population, and to hold a dramatically lower share of baccalaureate degrees than the rest of the population. While we need to raise the bar for all learners in the United States to ensure that our future workforce can compete in a global economy, Indian Country students have higher hurdles than most in order to successfully compete.

There are challenges specific to doing business in Indian Country. But it is also clear that tribes have and continue to take steps to address economic development issues. For example:

- Many tribes, such as the Navajo Nation, Muscogee Creek Nation, Pullayup Tribes and Shoshone Bannock, have developed sophisticated judicial and legal systems.
- Tribes continue to develop disciplined strategic plans.
- Developing infrastructure, whether that involves roads, schools or utilities, remains a high priority. Strong infrastructure is essential for tribal members' quality of life as well as economic development.
- Tribal human capital is improving. There are increasing numbers of Native American professionals in law, medicine and finance who are contributing to their communities.
- There's continuing focus on developing stronger working relationships with multi-jurisdictional interests such as cities, counties, states and federal entities.

Tribes and the private sector must develop mutually acceptable terms on several issues in order to attract capital. Some key terms are:

- The tribe must duly authorize the proposed relationship between the tribe and the private sector.
- The tribe and the private sector need clear and enforceable business and credit agreements.
- The tribe and private sector must develop disputes resolution processes. This entails tribes and the private sector developing mutually acceptable agreements on sovereign immunity and, choice of law.

In short, there are still obstacles tribal governments must overcome in order to attract consistent and appropriate investment interest.

For example, by transferring authority to tribes and streamlining the review process, as is proposed in the recommended enhancements of the Indian Tribal Energy Development and Self-Determination Act Amendments of 2014, the government can help Indian Country more easily attract interest from energy development.

More generally, I believe the Federal Government, Indian Country leadership and the private sector can work together on steps to increase investment potential.

Government needs to continue to identify simple and accountable ways to reduce federal review and/or approvals and to continue the responsible transfer of authority to Indian Country leadership.

Government can facilitate economic development by supporting existing incentives such as New Market Tax Credits, Low-Income Housing Tax Credits and Tribal Economic Development Bonds.

Indian Country leadership has an important role to play by staying focused on developing judicial and legislative capacity and basic infrastructure. It is imperative that Indian Country leadership obtain stakeholder support and that stakeholders' interests are aligned with the interests of their respective tribes. Finally, tribal leadership should engender cooperation between tribes, impacted communities and businesses to develop and execute investment strategies.

In closing, I want to note that KeyBank believes in helping all of our communities to thrive, including our Indian Country communities. Reducing the review process and creating more autonomy for tribes to attract investment by the private sector will enhance the ability of Indian Country leaders to help their own communities to thrive.

With experience in Indian Country, the private sector will come to understand that Indian Country is a dynamic place to do business, that mutually acceptable terms can be developed that build Indian Country economic independence and sustainable quality of life for Native America.

Thank you again for your time and attention to this very important issue, and I would be happy to answer your questions.

Senator BARRASSO. Thank you very much, Mr. Lettig. We appreciate your testimony. Thanks for joining us today.

Mr. Sherman, welcome to the Committee. If I could ask you to present your testimony.

STATEMENT OF GERALD SHERMAN, VICE CHAIRMAN, NATIVE CDFI NETWORK

Mr. SHERMAN. Chairman Tester, Vice Chairman Barrasso and members of the Senate Committee on Indian Affairs, thank you for this opportunity to testify.

My name is Gerald Sherman, I am an Oglala Lakota, and I grew up on the Pine Ridge Indian Reservation in South Dakota. Today my home is in Red Lodge, Montana. I have been working for over 20 years in finance and banking in Indian Country. Most recently, I have been the President of Indian Land Capital Company, where I did full faith and credit lending to tribes to buy lands. ILCC's unique lending methods work well for tribes.

I am here today on behalf of the Native CDFI network. Our mission is to be a national voice and advocate that strengthens and promotes Native Community Development Financial Institutions, creating access to capital and resources for Native peoples. In my testimony today, I would like to cover three things: one, the unmet demand for investments in Indian Country; two, how CDFIs can serve as conduits for those investments; and three, how policy makers can help to improve the environment in which Native CDFIs operate in order to strengthen the role they play in stimulating Native economies.

First, the unmet demand for investments in Indian Country. As you know, Native communities experience substantially higher rates of poverty and unemply9ment than mainstream America and face a unique set of challenges to economic growth, including a lack of basic financial services.

A recent FDIC study revealed that 41.3 percent of Native households are under-banked and 14.5 percent of Native households are completely unbanked. Also, the Treasury Department estimates an unmet capital need in Native communities of about $44 billion.

So how are Native CDFIs serving as a conduit for Indian Country investments? Native CDFIs are filling the credit and capital gaps not met by traditional lenders and investors and provide a viable alternative to predatory lenders. They have been working to create innovative solutions to economic development barriers and are beginning to show impact.

One example of the impact that Native CDFIs can have on tribal economies is evidenced by a 2009 study of Lakota Funds, one of the longest standing CDFIs operating on the Pine Ridge Indian Reservation. The Small Business Economics Journal published a study showing the positive impact of Lakota Funds over a 19-year time frame on the quality of life on the reservation. They found that Lakota Funds succeeded in raising per capita income, creating social benefits and contributing to household and community success.

In order to continue to build on the successful impact that Native CDFIs have had on their local economies, the Native CDFI network respectfully presents the following recommendations. First, we urge Congress to fund the fiscal year 2015 NACA appropriations at $15 million. We would like to re cognize Senator Tom Udall from New Mexico for his strong support of Native CDFIs. He has championed the first increase in the NACA appropriations since fiscal year 2009. We appreciate his efforts as well as the support from Chairman Tester, Senator Tim Johnson from South Dakota, and the rest of your colleagues on the Senate Appropriations Committee.

Second, we encourage Congress to make the waiver for the loan Federal match requirement permit for the NACA financial institution assistance program in the CDFI Fund. Given the economic conditions in Indian Country, Native CDFIs faced bigger hurdles than their non-Native counterparts in accessing private sector funding from corporate and philanthropic sources as well as individual donors. We propose that USDA create a pilot intermediary re-lending program that allows Native CDFIs to access mortgage capital through the Rural Development Section 502 loan program.

Fourth, we urge the CDFI Fund to implement its non-guaranty program so that it is accessible to Native CDFIs. The Native CDFI Network and its partners have been working to identify strategies to ensure full participation by Native CDFIs and Indian Country. In particular, we urge the CDFI Fund to ensure that the alternative forms of collateral are eligible to secure lending under the bond program, including lease-hold mortgages.

Finally, we encourage the CDFI Fund to implement the new market tax credit program in a way that maximizes the flow of capital to Indian Country. We were pleased to see yesterday that the CDFI Fund is launching a new capacity-building initiative to educate minority and community development entities.

In conclusion, I would like to recognize our relationship with the CDFI Fund staff for their commitment to the growth and stability of the Native CDFI industry. We appreciate the willingness to work toward fitting the programs into Indian Country rather than requiring Indian Country to fit into their programs.

I would also like to thank you, Mr. Chairman, for this opportunity to present the testimony of the Native CDFI network. We look forward to working with you and the Committee to continue to explore ways to improve the economic conditions in Native communities. Thank you.

[The prepared statement of Mr. Sherman follows:]

PREPARED STATEMENT OF GERALD SHERMAN, VICE CHAIRMAN, NATIVE CDFI NETWORK

Introduction

Chairman Tester, Vice Chairman Barrasso, and members of the Senate Committee on Indian Affairs—thank you for this opportunity to testify at this oversight hearing on *Economic Development: Encouraging Investment in Indian Country.* My name is Gerald Sherman. I am an Oglala Lakota, and I grew up on the Pine Ridge Indian Reservation in South Dakota. Today, my home is in Roscoe, MT.

I have been working for over 20 years to encourage investment in Indian Country. I am the founding board chairman and first executive director of the Lakota Funds, a community development loan fund on the Pine Ridge Reservation and one of the first micro-enterprise loan funds in the U.S. My banking career also included working with Norwest Bank (now Wells Fargo Bank), where I worked in commercial lending and as manager of a bank on the Lower Brule Reservation in South Dakota. I also worked for the Federal Reserve Bank of Minneapolis and later for First Interstate BancSystem of Montana where my focus was on increasing banking services to Indian Nations and low-income communities, and managing the bank's Community Reinvestment Act efforts.

In 2005, I worked with the Indian Land Tenure Foundation to create the the Indian Land Capital Company (ILCC), a national financial institution that makes loans to tribal governments to purchase alienated lands and fractionated ownership interests in trust lands. As the President and CEO, I have helped to deploy over $7 million in loans. ILCC views and deals with tribes as sovereign nations. It works toward changing the way traditional lenders view lending to Indian nations, demonstrating that these are credit-worthy, sophisticated political and economic entities that represent good business opportunities. Whereas tribes are treated merely as corporate entities by some lenders, ILCC views them as sovereigns and, as such, lends to them in a way that respects their sovereign status.

I am here today on behalf of the Native CDFI Network (NCN), which is a coalition of Native CDFIs and partners. Our mission is to be a national voice and advocate that strengthens and promotes Native community development financial institutions, creating access to capital and resources for Native peoples. Formed in 2009, the organization unifies Native CDFIs serving American Indian, Alaska Native, and Native Hawaiian communities. Our purpose is to create opportunities to assess the relative successes and challenges of serving distressed markets, identify our collective priorities, and strengthen our industry.

The Native CDFI Network is led by a Board of Directors comprised of nine dedicated leaders and practitioners within the Native CDFI industry. Members of the Board inform the Network's organizational growth and development by directing committee initiatives designed to maximize our impact while engaging our membership base. In addition, the Native CDFI Network's Board includes two Ex Officio seats filled by representatives of long-established national community development organizations.

In my testimony today, I would like to cover three things: (1) the unmet demand for investments in Indian Country, (2) how Native community development financial institutions or CDFIs serve as conduits for investments in Indian Country, and (3) how policy makers can help to improve the environment in which Native CDFIs operate in order to strengthen the role they play in stimulating Native economies.

The Umet Demand for Investments in Indian Country

As you know, Native communities experience substantially higher rates of poverty and unemployment than mainstream America and face a unique set of challenges to economic growth. Lack of physical, legal, and telecommunications infrastructure; access to affordable financial products and services; and limited workforce development strategies are common challenges that Native entrepreneurs, homebuyers, and consumers face and must overcome in order to be successful in their local economy.

According to the U.S. Department of the Treasury's 2001 Native American Lending Study, 86 percent of Native communities lack access to a single financial institution (with a broad definition that includes a simple ATM), and 15 percent of tribal citizens need to travel over 100 miles to access a financial institution.[1] Financial institutions with American Indian, Alaska Native, and Native Hawaiian communities in their service areas clearly have not adequately met the needs of these communities. The geographic boundaries of Indian reservations, confusion about tribal sovereignty, and an historic lack of access to credit and financial services in Native communites have caused many financial institutions to overlook these potential market segments. This lack of financial services has had a severe economic impact in underserved Native communities across Indian Country.

A recent Federal Deposit Insurance Corporation (FDIC) study revealed that 41.3 percent of American Indian and Alaska Native households are underbanked, and 14.5 percent of American Indian and Alaska Native households are completely unbanked.[2] This limited access to basic financial services in Native communities highlights the work left to be done to connect Native people to the benefits of the American financial system. The Treasury Department estimates an unmet capital need in Native communities of $44 billion.[3]

---

[1] Department of the Treasury, (2001) *Native American Lending Study*, *http:// www.cdfifund.gov/docs/2001*lnactallendinglstudy.pdf.
[2] 2011 FDIC National Survey of Unbanked and Underbanked Households (September 2012), accessed at *http://www.fdic.gov/householdsurvey/2012*lunbankedreport.pdf, p.15.
[3] Treasury, 2001.

How Native CDFIs Can Serve as a Conduit for Investments in Indian Country

CDFIs are private-sector, financial intermediaries with community development as their primary mission. While CDFIs share a common mission, they have a variety of structures and development lending goals. There are six basic types of CDFIs: community development banks, community development loan funds, community development credit unions, microenterprise funds, community development corporation-based lenders and investors, and community development venture capital funds. All are market-driven, locally-controlled, private-sector organizations. CDFIs measure success by focusing on the "double bottom line:" economic gains and the contributions they make to the local community.[4]

There are 831 certified CDFIs in existence across the United States. Of those, 68 are certified Native CDFIs, which means that they are entities that primarily serve a Native community, i.e., at least 50 percent of its activities are directed toward serving American Indians, Alaska Natives and/or Native Hawaiians. The 68 certified Native CDFIs are located in 21 states, including four in Montana. There are approximately 60 emerging Native CDFIs across Indian Country preparing for certification. The Native CDFI industry's rapid growth is a direct response to the lack of access to conventional financial services in Indian Country.

In the short term, Native CDFIs are filling the credit and capital gaps in Indian Country left by traditional lenders and investors. In the long term, they are grooming Native consumers, entrepreuners, and potential homebuyers to access traditional lenders in the future. They have been working to create innovative solutions to overcome economic development barriers and are beginning to show impact:

Developing Economies and Building Assets Native CDFIs have proven themselves as vehicles towards developing healthy, vibrant Native economies and communities. They have entered markets normally considered "high-risk" and have been responsible for an astounding transformation—serving as the catalyst for developing local economies, building assets, and reducing persistent poverty.

Native CDFIs' programs and services are designed to help their clients, who are otherwise underserved, to build individual financial assets and savings skills so that they have access to mainstream economic opportunities such as homeownership, education, and small business creation, as well as cultural assets such as regalia for ceremonies, traditional foods and gardens, or items necessary for subsistence.

Here are some examples of the positive impact some Native CDFIs have had:

Lakota Funds, Oglala Sioux Tribe, SD

A 2009 study of the work of the Lakota Funds shows specific examples of economic impact. The *Small Business Economics* journal published a study by four university economists in April 2009 showing strong and consistent positive impact of the Lakota Funds on the quality of life on the Pine Ridge Indian Reservation. They concluded:

> The Lakota Funds succeeded in raising real per capita income of Shannon county residents consistently and significantly throughout the 1987–2006 study period. . .[thus showing how] a well-designed and highly successful micro-enterprise financing structure can confer large and significant private and social benefits. . .sustained growth in real incomes. . .net wealth and further personal, household, and community successes in socio-economic, health. . ., educational. . ., and other dimensions of progressive quality living.[5]

Four Bands Community Fund, Cheyenne River Sioux Tribe, SD

Four Bands Community Fund provides another example of the economic impact that a Native CDFI can have on its community. Four Bands is a non-profit, Native CDFI serving the Cheyenne River Indian Reservation, which is about the size of the State of Connecticut. Founded in 2000, Four Bands' mission is to create economic opportunity by helping people build strong and sustainable small businesses and increase their financial capability to create assets and wealth. Since it began providing services, this small CDFI has assisted nearly 5000 customers which is 60 percent of the reservation's population. This includes $4.2 million credit builder and small business loans, creating or retaining 440 jobs, helping 520 individuals complete financial literacy training, sponsoring 150 youth entrepreuner inters, and exposing 2,500 students to the concepts of financial literacy and entrepreneurship.

---

[4] http://www.cdfi.org/about-cdfis/what-are-cdfis/.

[5] Benson, D; Lies, A; Okunade, A; and Wunnava, P, "Economic impact of a private sector micro-financing scheme in South Dakota," (2009), accessed at http://www.lakotafunds.org/docs/SDmicrofinance.pdf.

Financial Capability and Inclusion Financial education opportunities provided by Native CDFIs have helped clients—both adults and youth—to improve their access to conventional financial services such as consumer loans, mortgages, tax preparation services, and small business credit. They have also allowed them to enter the financial mainstream more competitively with better rates and fees, based on improved credit scores and history. They have provided a viable alternative to predatory lenders who prey on uneducated consumers and trap them into cycles of high-cost debt and other financial products.

Native American Community Development Corporation, Blackfeet Indian Reservation, MT

The Native American Community Development Corporaton started the Mini-Bank Program in 1996 in Browning, Montana at the Browning Middle School. Since its inception, the Blackfeet "Mini-Bank" has garnered interest from many schools and institutions around the State of Montana and the nation. Now serving six reservations in three states, the Mini-Bank program currently has more than 670 youth accounts with more than $40,000 in their savings accounts. This Native CDFI believes that young people should be taught early in life that financial literacy equals economic empowerment. Their program helps youth develop good saving habits and gives them the confidence and independence to make sound financial decisions. Builidng financial capability of youth is a key to building wealth and economic prosperity in Native communities.

Policy Recommendations to Strenghthen the Role Native CDFIs Play in Stimulating Native Economies

In order to continue to build on the successful impact that Native CDFI's have had on their local economies, the Native CDFI Network respectfully presents the following general and specific recommendations to policy makers.

Generally, we encourage federal and state policy makers to recognize the unique land, legal, and jurisdictional issues in Indian Country when implementing their community and economic development programs. Native efforts may not fit into existing programs and may require flexibility, exceptions, or innovative pilot programs. In some cases, the need in Indian Country may be so severe that competitive government programs should include extra points or designated set-asides specifically for efforts serving Native communities. The CDFI Fund's Native American CDFI Assistance (NACA) program is a perfect example of a Native-focused program designed by the Treasury Department to meet the capital and credit needs identified by its Native American Lending Study in 2001.[6]

Specifically, we would like to offer the following recommendations:

1. Fund FY 15 NACA Appropriations at $15 million.

We would like to recognize Senator Tom Udall from New Mexico for his strong support of the work of Native CDFIs. As Chairman of the Senate Appropriations Committee on Financial Services and General Government, he has championed the first increase in NACA appropriations under the Treasury's CDFI Fund since FY 2009. We appreciate his efforts as well as the support from you, Chairman Tester, Senator Tim Johnson from South Dakota, and the rest of your colleagues on the Senate Appropriations Committee.

We urge Congress to continue to fund the Native American CDFI Assistance Initiative program at the $15 million level in the FY 2015 Appropriations bill because (1) Native CDFIs can help to address the unmet financial services and capital need in Native communities, (2) the demand for NACA funds from certified and emerging CDFIs continues to sky rocket—over double the available funds in FY 13, and (3) the economic impact of Native CDFIs is significant.

2. Make the waiver for the non-federal match requirement permanent for the NACA Financial Assistance program.

The Native CDFI Network urges Congress to reinstate and make permanent the waiver for the non-federal match requirement for Treasury's CDFI Fund Native American CDFI Assistance Financial Assistance program. This recommendation is based on the unique status and characteristics of Indian Country and Native CDFIs.

The CDFI Fund acknowledged the challenges to raising non-federal match for Native CDFIs in its *Native Initiatives Strategic Plan for FY 2009—2014*, which identified as a key strategy to "Increase Opportunities for Native CDFIs to Access Available Capital:"

---

[6] Treasury, 2001.

The Native American Lending Study identified the lack of lending capital as one of the greatest barriers to economic development in Native Communities, and securing capital remains one the most significant challenges Native CDFIs face. The NACA Program's Financial Assistance component requires. . .the CDFI to match the award amount dollar for dollar with non-Federal funds. Meeting this non-Federal match requirement can be difficult for Native CDFIs because, for most Native communities, Federal agencies are the main source of funds. As a result, the requirement may undermine the ability of some Native CDFIs to secure capital through the NACA Program or may even discourage them from applying. In 2009–2014, the CDFI Fund will explore ways to increase opportunities for Native CDFIs to access available capital. [7]

The following are key factors that make raising non-federal matching funds especially challenging for Native CDFIs.

Economic Conditions

Indian Country continues to struggle through an economic downturn. Congress waived non-federal match requirements for NACA from FY09 to FY13 during the recession. While there have been some signs of recovery in Indian Country, many tribal communities are in persistent poverty counties where ongoing investment and opportunities are necessary. The ability of Native CDFIs to access NACA without a non-federal match is a strategy that was working well to overcome significant economic barriers.

Economic indicators in Indian Country have always lagged the mainstream U.S. economy. For example, according to the Economic Policy Institute, "Although the Great Recession is technically over, when looking at the American Indian employment situation, there is little sign of recovery. Nationally, Native American unemployment continues to rise, and employment continues to decline." [8] Making the NACA match waiver permanent would ensure that Native CDFIs are using scarce dollars more efficiently to create jobs.

Philanthropic Environment

Native CDFIs face bigger hurdles than their non-Native counterparts to accessing private sector funding from corporate and philanthropic sources, as well as individual donors. This is evident historically and even more so in the wake of the recession. According to a report published by the Foundation Center and Native Americans in Philanthropy in 2011, U.S. foundation support explicitly targeting Native Americans declined as a share of total foundation giving from 2000–2009. [9] While mainstream CDFIs are able to raise their match through long-standing relationships with private sector partners, most Native communities do not have these sources because they are isolated and do not have local wealth available to their communities. Making the NACA match waiver permanent would allow Native CDFIs to build their capacity to establish these relationships going forward.

Organizational Capacity

Many NCDFIs are small and emerging, and, as a result, may not have a fundraiser on staff or board members with fundraising experience to raise monies from non-federal sources. To create a strong balance sheet, emerging CDFIs need equity (not debt) at early stage of development. Without access to NACA, many emerging and newly certified Native find it difficult to attract other capital. Non-federal resources are precious and often Native CDFIs are torn between using non-federal funding to attractive several different funding sources. This becomes an unproductive juggling act.

NACA is the most common source of equity for all Native CDFIs. This equity is being leveraged by more established Native CDFIs with the wherewithal to qualify for private sector debt.

  3. Launch a pilot mortgage intermediary relending program that allows Native CDFIs to access mortgage capital through the U.S. Department of Agriculture's Rural Development Section 502 Direct and Guaranteed Loan Program.

---

[7] Department of the Treasury—CDFI Fund, (2009), Native Initiatives Strategic Plan for Fiscal Years 2009–2014, *http://cdfifund.gov/docs/2009/naca/Native%20American%20Strategic%20Plan.pdf.*

[8] Algernon Austin, (2010), "Different Race, Different Recession: American Indian Unemployment in 2010." *http://www.epi.org/page/-/pdf/ib289.pdf?nocdn=1*

[9] Mukai, Reina and Lawrence, Steven (2011), "Foundation Funding for Native American Issues and Peoples," *http://www.nativephilanthropy.org/*

The Single Family Housing Direct and Guaranteed Loan Program (502) is successfully bringing mortgage capital to rural communities across America. Unfortunately, its success on Native trust land has been limited. Native CDFIs are perfectly situated to partner with Rural Development personnel to improve the outreach and delivery of the program.

We urge USDA Rural Development to launch a pilot program in Indian Country to allow Native CDFIs to be guaranteed lenders under the 502 Guaranteed Loan Program and intermediary lenders under the 502 Direct Loan Program.

4. Implement the CDFI Fund Bond Guarantee Program so that it is accessible to Native CDFIs.

The Native CDFI Network, Opportunity Finance Network, Native American Finance Officers Association, and CDFIs across the country interested in making the CDFI Bond Guarantee Program successful have been working closely with the CDFI Fund to improve the viability of the program in Indian Country. Our talks have focused on common sense adaptations to the existing program structure to allow for broader CDFI participation. We are happy to report that we have made some progress with the CDFI Fund, but we are continuing to identify strategies to ensure full participation by Native CDFIs and Indian Country.

In particular, we urge the CDFI Fund to ensure that that alternate forms of collateral are eligible to secure lending under the Bond Program. This would assist Native CDFIs as they originate loans to small businesses and other entities. It would be helpful for the CDFI Fund to confirm that Leasehold Equity Mortgages are acceptable forms of collateral.

Additionally, there is ambiguity over the application of the Principle Loss Collateral Provision (PLCP). This provision enables third parties to provide a guarantee in instances where there is insufficient collateral. While the CDFI Fund will allow tribes to provide the PLCP for tribal applicants (so long as they are deemed sufficiently separate), entities which provide the PLCP must be publicly rated as investment grade. If an entity is not publicly rated (as is the case for many tribes), their credit worthiness is assessed by the Fund, which ultimately decides whether they are eligible to provide the PLCP. It would be helpful to have more information about this evaluation process. What methods are used? Are tribes evaluated like any other non-publicly rated entity?

Finally, there is uncertainty among the Eligible CDFIs and Qualified Issuers as to whether they can amend their capital distribution plans to accommodate tribal applicants. We encourage the CDFI Fund to provide greater clarity on the matter.

5. Implement the CDFI Fund New Markets Tax Credit Program to maximize the flow of capital to Indian Country.

The CDFI Fund New Markets Tax Credit (NMTC) Program has great potential to bring capital to Indian Country. To maximize its effectiveness, we recommend the following:

- The CDFI Fund should require that NMTC allocation application reviewers reading applications from Community Development Entities (CDEs) with the primary mission of serving Native communities have experience working in these communities. If that is not possible, then all such applications should be read by CDFI Fund Native Initiatives staff and not outside contractors.
- The NMTC allocation application allows applicants to commit to serve states that have received disproportionately low levels of NMTC investment ("underserved states"). American Indian, Alaska Native and Native Hawaiian communities should be considered equivalent to "underserved states" since they too have low levels of NMTC investments.

6. Expand the Community Reinvestment Act (CRA) to encourage investments in Native communities and Native CDFIs that serve them.

The federal bank regulators should expand the CRA regulations to explicitly recognize lending, services, and investments in Indian Country. In particular, bank examiners should place a higher value on mortgage lending activity on tribal trust lands in order to provide incentive to lenders that have heretofore met their Native American goals by lending to tribal members living in urban areas or other non-trust lands.

Conclusion

I'd like to thank you, Mr. Chairman, for this opportunity to present the testimony of the Native CDFI Network. We look forward to working with you and the Committee to improve the economic conditions across Indian Country.

The CHAIRMAN. [Presiding] Mr. Allis, you are up.

STATEMENT OF KEVIN J. ALLIS, EXECUTIVE DIRECTOR, NATIVE AMERICAN CONTRACTORS ASSOCIATION

Mr. ALLIS. Thank you, Chairman Tester. I would like to thank you and the honorable members of the Senate Indian Affairs Committee for allowing me to come here and testify today. It truly is a pleasure and I know that there are many people sitting behind me that deserve to be up here as well and are worth noting: the leaders of the Native American Finance Officers Association, those at the American Indian Chamber of Commerce in California, in Arizona, South Carolina; National Indian Gaming Association all have had a lot of input on this and all are boots-on-the-ground organizations that do great things for Indian Country. To be here is wonderful.

Economic development and discussion of economic development is an important issue and has been for decades. Regular dialogue is necessary and this is a warmly welcomed opportunity to speak to it.

For the birth of the present day era of self-determination, we can look back to President Nixon in 1970. Back then, he recognized Indian Country as being the most deprived and most isolated minority group in the Nation. Although since 1970 there has been great improvement and a lot of really cool things have happened, a lot of work needs to be done. Certainly, Indian Country has a whole has challenges with respect to access to capital and access to financial investment and resources. But unless the valuable investments that Congress has made in the past are safeguarded and protected and attended to, some of the new initiatives that we discuss today and consider in the future likely could woefully fail. When I speak to that, the importance of vibrant tribal communities are certainly attractive places for investment. If we can maintain that and continue to grow those tribal communities, we will see great things happen in Indian Country.

I speak specifically to the investment that Congress has made in allowing Indian tribes, Alaska Native corporations, Native Hawaiian organizations to operate in the SBA 8(a) program. Support of this program and our participation in this program is enormously important. These are programs that can do and can continue to provide critically needed resources to some of the most remote Native communities across the Country.

Indian gaming has been a wonderful thing for Indian Country. I am a tribal member of the Forest County Potawatomi Community in Wisconsin. My mother grew up on an Indian reservation, my grandfather Harry Ritchie and my great-grandfather Henry Ritchie were great tribal leaders of our community. If they could see today what Indian gaming has done, they would be amazed.

But not all tribes are lucky like ours and located near metropolitan areas. Most of our communities live in very rural, remote areas of the Country, not near major metropolitan areas. Our brothers and sisters in Alaska are in some of the most rural areas in the world. And these communities desperately need resources to continue to flow into those areas so they can achieve self-determination and a way of life that the rest of the Country is able to experience in this great Nation.

So we need to continue to give attention to programs like the SBA 8(a) program, because it doesn't matter where your tribe is located, it doesn't matter where your Native community is located. Valuable resources can still come into your community in a way that makes a big difference.

In allowing tribes to really get involved in the 8(a) program, Congress recognized that providing access to the Federal marketplace would spawn business development for tribal businesses that would produce great results. The purchasing power of the Federal Government would not only advance important social issues that were built into the 8(a) program, but would also fuel increased competition thereby expanding and diversifying the sources of goods and services that the Federal Government procures. This is a win-win for both the Federal Government and Indian Country.

Back in 1987 and 1988, this Committee looked at this issue, then chaired by the great Senator Inouye. Relying on a study commissioned by then-President Ronald Reagan, they looked at this issue and brilliantly recognized the inherent value that by ensuring access to Federal contracting for Indian Country, Native enterprises could grow and solve problems for both their communities and make taxpayer money be efficiently spent.

These programs offer an extremely efficient and wise use of taxpayer dollars. We all know how important that is in today's world. These types of hands-up programs, instead of a handout program, are the types of things we need to look at from the top to the bottom. That is what the 8(a) program is. It is exchanging goods and services to the Federal Government in exchange for valuable resources that fund programs. Recently, Section 811 of the National Defense Authorization Act has severely impacted Indian Country and has caused a decline in direct awards to over $20 million and close to $2.5 billion. That is a lot of money that has left our neighborhood, our communities, that goes to fund programs that move us toward self-determination. We really need you, Senator, and the rest of your Committee, to reach upon your colleagues in other committees and to really look at the types of things that have happened in Indian Country with respect to the devastating impact of Section 811.

Thank you very much for your time.

[The prepared statement of Mr. Allis follows:]

PREPARED STATEMENT OF KEVIN J. ALLIS, EXECUTIVE DIRECTOR, NATIVE AMERICAN CONTRACTORS ASSOCIATION

Good Afternoon, Honorable Chairman Tester, Vice Chairman Barrasso, and Members of the Committee. My name is Kevin Allis, and I am a tribal member of the Forest County Potawatomi Community located in the State of Wisconsin. I come from a family whose mother grew up on our reservation, and whose grandfather and great-grandfather served as the Chairman of our tribe. Today I proudly serve as the Executive Director of the Native American Contractors Association, and the Board Chairman of the Potawatomi Business Development Corporation. In both capacities, my goals are to ensure that Native Americans are able to enjoy the many things this great nation has to offer, while still being able to preserve their traditions, languages, and customary ways of life. It has never been lost on me, and I'm certain my ancestors, that every minute we live that is dedicated to improving the lives of millions we will never meet is tremendous. I know that each of you understand and experience everyday this same kind of responsibility, and go to bed each night knowing that the hard work of the day will make someone else's life a little better.

I would to thank you for holding this hearing, and allowing for me to testify. Economic development within Indian Country is an important issue, and regular dialogue and consideration of the issue is absolutely necessary. The present day era of self-determination was birthed in large measure by President Richard Nixon, who in a special message before Congress on July 8, 1970 stated, "The first Americans, the Indians, are the most deprived and most isolated minority group in our nation on virtually every scale of measurement; unemployment, income, education, health-the condition of Indian people ranks at the bottom."

Although conditions have greatly improved since 1970, much work remains to be done. Efforts and programs that exist today must be improved, and at the very least, remain fully intact, so their intended designs, which are to improve the lives of Native Americans and ability to control their own destinies, is realized. Today's hearing looks at "Economic Development: Encouraging Investment in Indian Country." There is no doubt that Indian Country, like other minority communities, has challenges with respect to access to capital. However, unless there are other viable programs to put such precious investment of capital to use, accomplishing long-term sustainability is difficult. The existence of time tested and proven programs, in which Native communities can invest, and thus parlay the value of such capital is critical in the achievement of Native sustainable self-determination. Two extremely effective federal Indian programs have been Native participation in the Small Business Administration (SBA) 8(a) Business Development Program ("SBA 8(a) Program"), and the Indian Incentive Program (IIP). It is here that Native communities, large and small, rural or urban, have been able to move closer to achieving the goal of self-determination.

SBA 8(a) Program

The SBA 8(a) Program was enacted during the 1960s to assist eligible small economically and socially disadvantaged business concerns to compete in the American economy through federal contracting. Recognizing that small businesses are critical to our economy, the SBA is charged with assisting and protecting their interests. Congress found that by providing access to the federal procurement market, the business development of small business concerns of the disadvantaged could be achieved. America has a long history of using its purchasing power as a means to further the business development of various individuals and groups who would otherwise be excluded from the huge government contracting market. This not only furthers important social goals, but fuels increased competition, thereby expanding and diversifying the sources of supplies and products. Native enterprises are starting to use these procurement programs just as the government intended, and in doing so, are developing business approaches and models that are building strong Native economies; thus fostering the realization of self-determination.

In fact, in hearings held by this Committee in 1987 and 1988, it was found that including Indian tribes and Alaska Native-owned firms in government contracting was a wonderful way to address the important needs of Native communities. This Committee relied upon President Ronald Reagan's, "Commission on Indian Reservations Economies," which had documented that the government's procurement policies were significant obstacles to economic development, yet if crafted correctly, could provide attractive benefits for both the Native American population and the Federal Government. In 1983, President Ronald Reagan commissioned this report to determine how the economies of Indian reservations could be improved. The Commission produced a report in 1984 that provided several recommendations to improve reservation economies, based on parameters established by the President's statement on American Indian policy. One of the key recommendations made by the Commission was to create avenues to increase the participation of Indian tribes (including Alaska Native Corporations) in the federal contracting marketplace through the SBA 8(a) Program.

The Commission provided several reasons to open federal contracting opportunities to Native Americans. First, it was determined that the increased use of Native business concerns in federal procurement would not require any new federal funds. It would draw upon the existing budgets of government agencies for the purchase of goods and services. Importantly, it would be an effort that simply does not just give money to Indians, but instead, improves access of Native-owned firms to the federal marketplace, and allow them the opportunity to earn their way. This is the classic "hand-up" approach, instead of one that is merely of a "hand-out" methodology. This situation creates a "win-win" scenario for both the Federal Government and the Native community. It results in an extremely efficient use of valuable taxpayer dollars, which in these times is extremely important. In addition, the Commission found that federal agencies would not be disadvantaged because the Native American suppliers would have to meet the quality, delivery, and cost requirements dictated by the missions of the agencies. While these two quotes are only a snapshot of the commission's report, they capture the reasoning behind the Commission recommending that the government allow Native American participation in the SBA 8(a) Program, as it was seen as logical and cost effective way to meet the needs and challenges of Native Americans across the country.

During the 1988 hearing, Chairman Inouye stated that, "directing the purchasing power of the Federal Government to accomplish social goals such as assisting disadvantaged members of society is well established," and he then noted that unfortunately, "this public policy goal has not been achieved with respect to the participation of businesses owned by Native Americans." This fact, in tandem with recognition of the unique trust obligation the Federal Government has with Native Americans acknowledged in the Constitution, federal laws, and by the Supreme Court, led Congress to enact legislation that opened the federal contracting marketplace to Indian Country. Today we refer to this program as the Native 8(a) program.

By creating unique Native 8(a) provisions, Congress recognized the special needs and its obligations to Indian Tribes, Alaska Native Corporations, and later Native Hawaiians Organizations. Like other 8(a) firms, Native business concerns can only participate in the SBA 8(a) Program through small businesses that are subject to stringent program entry eligibility requirements. Native enterprises have two key unique 8(a) provisions: (1) the competitive thresholds that limit the amount of sole-source awards do not apply; and (2) Native enterprises can participate in the SBA 8(a) Program through more than one company. This was the intent of Congress, and makes sense in light of the economic and social disadvantages with which Native communities must contend, and the number of Native Americans in need within these communities. The disadvantages suffered by Native Americans encompass entire communities and villages, as opposed to individuals who are socially and economically disadvantaged. The ability to operate more than one company, and perform on larger contracts, provides the necessary level of resources, through net profits, that can make a difference in changing large Native communities.

For years Native enterprises have provided quality services and cost effective products to the Federal Government. This has translated to resources being made available to Native communities that not only are used to fix systemic problems that have plagued Indian Country, but allows for these communities to preserve their culture, traditions, languages, and customary ways of life. However, in recent years, this all has been threatened. With unfair scrutiny, and devastating new provisions and regulations, Native contracting has seen a sharp decline over the past five (5) years. Section 811 of the 2010 National Defense Authorization Act ("Section 811") has unfairly stigmatized and thus discriminated against Native federal contractors. Once again, a hurdle of the kind the Reagan Commission identified as a problem to Native participation in the federal marketplace is alive and well, and causing much disruption.

Section 811 requires a justification and approval process for direct awards greater than $20 million that are awarded to Native contractors. Apparently it was designed as an additional process to ensure value in these contracts. The Government Accountability Office (GAO) released its report titled, "Slow Start to Implementation of Justifications for 8(a) Sole Source Contracts." The findings in this report are extremely important to Native communities, because as mentioned, their involvement in the SBA 8(a) Program, through community-owned businesses, provides critically important financial resources that fund the distribution of needed benefits and services.

So why is the GAO report so disturbing to Indian Country? The report clearly shows that the implementation of Section 811 is shattering Native communities. Because of the inherent inequitableness of the provision, coupled with the confusion and inconsistency of its implementation, indispensably needed benefits and services for some of the poorest communities in this nation face the real possibility of inadequate funding. The report indicates that between FY 2010–FY 2011, 8(a) contracting dollars valued greater than $20 million decreased sixty percent (60 percent) decrease in a single year.

As mentioned, and just as troubling, was the discovery that certain agencies were employing Section 811 incorrectly and/or inconsistently. As an example, the report mentioned that an Army Corps contracting official understood Section 811 as a "cap" on the size of 8(a) awards. Consistently throughout the rule making process it was explained that Section 811 was NOT a cap, but simply a threshold that triggers a process to further ensure value. Right from the beginning NACA was worried that despite the explicit acknowledgment that Section 811 is not a cap, it would be interpreted as such. The report validates this concern. In addition, the report identified instances whereby agencies had established their own threshold limits, in a nonsensical manner, and without any consideration to the entities and the communities served by such entities, not to mention that such policies are inconsistent with federal law.

The 8(a) program for many Native Americans instills pride in communities that aspire to gain the business acumen essential to compete in the federal marketplace. Disadvantaged small businesses such as those owned by Tribes, Alaska Native Corporations, and Native Hawaiian Organizations may not be able to compete with other contractors without the business development tools provided by the SBA 8(a) Program. Section 811 is obstructing the growth of Native community-owned small businesses, which unlike ''individually'' owned entities, have more than one family to provide needed benefits and resources. The result of Section 811 is that millions of dollars have vanished from significantly needed services, benefits and programs for the national Native community with numbers over 4.5 million individuals. Up to this point in time, the SBA 8(a) Program has achieved success in boosting Native economies across the country where other programs have failed. Although Indian gaming may have some success in a few populated areas, federal contracting, through the SBA 8(a) Program, has consistently fueled rural and very poor Native communities. Section 811 threatens this success, and has now become a new highlight on the 200∂ year history of unfair burdens cast upon Native Americans.

This Committee and others should take a good look at the devastating impact Section 811 has inflicted upon Native communities. It is imperative that this matter be corrected, so that the intent of Congress with respect to Native enterprise participation in federal contracting is realized to its fullest extent.

Indian Incentive Program

A second and equally valuable program in the federal contracting marketplace has been the Indian Incentive Program (IIP). This program, just as the SBA 8(a) Program, not only create jobs across the country, it also represents an efficient use of taxpayer dollars. As noted, building and maintaining tribal economies through federal contracting programs is a sensible substitute for a welfare program that no doubt would be an expensive proposition. Just as important, like other programs aimed at helping Native Americans, IIP is based on the government-to-government relationship and federal trust responsibility to Native Americans.

Congress authorized the IIP in 1988 as an amendment to Indian Finance Act. The IIP was created to increase the utilization of Native American owned businesses into the federal contracting supply chain, by incentivizing larger businesses to use the valuable goods and services provided by Native-owned contractors. The program provides incentive payments of up to five percent (5 percent) when a prime contractor, or a subcontractor at any level in a procurement, utilizes a Native owned business as a subcontractor. When enacting the law, Congress explicitly left the program's funding decisions to the Appropriations Committee. Recognizing this program's value, Appropriators have funded the IIP, without interruption, since 1989.

The program has increased revenue for Native contractors, thereby successfully and efficiently leveraging a small line item many times over. Between fiscal years 1999–2010, the IIP leveraged cumulative program funding of $122 million into more than $2.5 billion in subcontractor revenue for Native businesses. According to the Department of Defense, the program has been utilized by more than 300 prime contractors, and more than 500 Native American subcontractors. It has been a successful tool to promote Native economic development, and again, is a program that represents the efficient and cost effective use of valuable taxpayer dollars.

The impact of this economic activity in Native communities has been significant. Native communities are often located in some of the most rural and isolated areas of the country, and lack access to any measurable amount of economic opportunity. Revenue generated through participation in the IIP provides a meaningful injection of capital into these communities in need. However, despite the program's success, some wish to see its progress halted. During consideration of FY13 appropriations, an amendment was filed to strip the modest $15 million available for the IIP.

We are keenly aware of the fiscal challenges faced by the Federal Government. While reducing wasteful spending in the defense budget is a widely shared goal, eliminating a program that has positively impacted Native-owned small businesses is not the way to achieve this goal. As mentioned, the program represents a brilliant use of taxpayer dollars in a way that fuels the economies of some of the poorest communities in this country. Efforts to eliminate such programs unfairly impacts small businesses that benefit from the modestly funded program, when much larger savings opportunities exist elsewhere. We ask that you support the IIP?s funding of $15 million, and greatly appreciate your efforts in speaking to your colleagues in the Senate on the need to preserve this program.

Conclusion

In sum, the communities which Native enterprises serve remain some of the poorest and most underserved groups in the United States. There is still tremendous work to be done in effecting positive and sustainable benefits for these communities. Approximately one percent (1 percent) of the federal contracting that Native community owned entities now receive is enabling the communities to create jobs and opportunities that are desperately needed. Through our self-reliance and business ingenuity, Native peoples are starting to provide for the self-sufficiency of our communities, thanks in large measure to programs like Native 8(a) and IIP. Keeping these are viable investment opportunities that Native communities can with confidence invest available capital is critical to the long term sustainability of Indian Country. The continued economic success and positive move towards self-determination require investment, access to capital, and the Native 8(a) program and IIP to remain intact as intended. We respectfully ask for this Committee to take a hard look at these programs, and the great value that both the Federal Government and Indian Country receive from their existence. The mere safeguarding of these two federal Indian programs is an investment in the Indian Country economic development.

I thank the Chairman, and the entire Committee for the opportunity to speak before you all today. I welcome any questions your Committee may have.

The CHAIRMAN. Thank you for your testimony.
Ms. Rupert, you are up.

STATEMENT OF SHERRY L. RUPERT, PRESIDENT, BOARD OF DIRECTORS, AMERICAN INDIAN ALASKA NATIVE TOURISM ASSOCIATION

Ms. RUPERT. Chairman Tester, Vice Chairman Barrasso, and members of the Senate Committee on Indian Affairs, thank you for the opportunity to appear this afternoon to discuss Indian Country tourism and its current and potential impact on Indian economic development and the United States.

The word tourism is an umbrella term for a vast canvas of travel, hospitality and vacation-related economic activities. No matter what name you call it, people stopping to spend time and spend money in Indian Country is a very significant opportunity for tribes and Native peoples to share and reinforce their cultures, generate income, create jobs and improve their quality of life.

As President of the board of directors of the only non-profit solely devoted to developing and sustaining Indian Country tourism, the American Indian Alaska Native Tourism Association, or AIANTA, provides technical assistance and training, creates and nurtures partnerships with Federal agencies, higher education institutions, the tourism industry and national Indian and non-Indian non-profits to leverage scarce available resources.

We provide these services through a cooperative agreement with the Bureau of Indian Affairs transportation division. This was authorized through the 1991 highway bill otherwise known as ISTEA. With support from Congress, we are working toward establishing a permanent program with a set budget within the reauthorization of MAP–21 so we can continue to help tribes build their capacity for tourism development. This has also led to an MOU with the Department of Interior and all of its bureaus.

International tourism is very important to Indian Country. According to a Department of Commerce survey, nearly 38 million overseas tourists visited the United States in 2013, and more than 1.5 million visited Indian Country. From 2011 to 2012, American Indian communities saw a significant increase in visitation from China, Australia and France. It is difficult gathering data for Indian Country, so we monitor the growing interest in Native-run operations and trips to our reservations.

I wanted to share a few success stories in Indian Country. First, the Standing Rock Sioux Tribe, which straddles North and South Dakota, operates hundreds of reservation tours every year. In 2013, eight Japanese visitors stayed six weeks and spent an average of $1,500 a day at Standing Rock. The tribe also offers limited buffalo hunts at $10,000 per customer. Icy Point Strait a majority-owned Native Alaskan business, operates 21 excursions in Icy Strait Point, a majority-owned Native Alaskan business, operates 21 excursions in Hoonah, Alaska, just 35 miles west of Juneau. The mostly Tlingit staff accommodated 69 cruise ships in 2013.

Monument Valley Simpson's Trailhandler Tours is a regular part of AIANTA's delegation to ITB Berlin, the second largest travel trade marketplace in the world. Specializing in tours of Southern Utah by Navajo guides who teach Navajo culture, the business welcomes between 80 and 100 people on an average summer night, mostly foreign tourists, and employs about 30 people year round.

So there is money to be made in Indian Country tourism. When that is better understood, more investment will follow. So to boost awareness, AIANTA is building an Indian Country destinations website to assist tribes, especially those tribes that are rural and remote. We are partnering with The George Washington University to create web-based training courses for tribal members to earn tourism certificates and a certification program. We are also partnering with our national American Indian associations such as the National Congress of American Indians, the National Indian Gaming Association, Native American Rights Fund, Southeast Tourism Society, Western States Policy Council, and National Geographic Society. We are working with them and they are supporting us in our efforts to build awareness, attract resources and encourage travel, tourism and recreation development in Indian Country.

Because of this intense interest in our culture, more and more tourists are coming to Indian Country. We are also seeing the industry take note. Tauck Tours, for example, is the largest and oldest tour company in North America. They are adding American Indian attractions and interpretation to their itineraries. Amtrak is also talking about adding more interpretation to their tours.

So in order to prepare for increased international visitation, Indian Country requires investment in tourism infrastructure and capacity building. We need to be ready for these millions of tourists that are coming to the United States and have an interest in us.

So how can you help? We would like to see greater coordination and collaboration between the Indian tourism programs across the Federal Government. We would also like to see a permanent tourism program authorized through the highway bill. We would like to give thanks to the Senator for writing the NATIVE Act, the Native American Tourism and Improving Visitor Experience Act, where it does all these things that I just mentioned, coordinating the Federal efforts, giving us a seat at the table with Brand USA. If we are going to market the United States, we need to include our tribes.

In conclusion, AIANTA's bottom line is this: if the Federal resources that currently exist for tourism were organized to be used collaboratively and made available to tribal governments, communities and businesses, the result would lead to more visitors, more income and more investment in Indian Country tourism. Mr. Chairman and members of the Committee, I thank you for your interest in tribal tourism and AIANTA's work. I thank you for including tourism in your exploration of investment in Indian Country economic development, and invite you to call upon AIANTA in the future as a resource.

[The prepared statement of Ms. Rupert follows:]

PREPARED STATEMENT OF SHERRY L. RUPERT, PRESIDENT, BOARD OF DIRECTORS, AMERICAN INDIAN ALASKA NATIVE TOURISM ASSOCIATION

Introduction

Chairman Tester, Vice Chairman Barrasso and Members of the Senate Committee on Indian Affairs, I thank you for the opportunity to appear before you today to discuss Indian Country tourism and its current and potential impact on Indian economic development in the United States.

The word "tourism" is an umbrella term for a vast canvas of travel, hospitality and vacation-related economic activities. No matter by what name you call it, people stopping to spend time and money in Indian Country—not just passing through—is a very significant opportunity for tribes and native peoples to share and reinforce their cultures, generate income, create jobs for adults and youth and improve their quality of life.

How do we build on tourism from its current base in Indian Country—help create the capacity to provide all the needed services, involve our communities in these decisions, inspire investment, build the infrastructure needed and keep our cultures alive and thriving? At the American Indian Alaska Native Tourism Association, we ask and try to answer these questions every day.

American Indian Alaska Native Tourism Association

As President of the Board of Directors, I have the honor of leading the Nation's only nonprofit solely devoted to developing and sustaining Indian Country tourism—the American Indian Alaska Native Tourism Association ("AIANTA" for short.) AIANTA's mission is to introduce the Nation's native peoples to a world where tourism has become a 181 billion dollar industry, the flow of visitors to Indian Country rapidly increasing from 3.5 percent (975,910) in 2011 to 4.7 percent (1.5 million) in 2013 according to the U.S. Department of Commerce. Expenditures for overseas visitors average $3,435 per trip.

From its beginning in 2002 as a volunteer group of American Indians and Alaska Natives and Native Hawaiians, AIANTA has grown into a recognized national leader in the tourism industry, included in the President's National Travel and Tourism Strategy. AIANTA is headquartered in Albuquerque, New Mexico, at the Indian Pueblo Cultural Center. In addition to leading AIANTA, I am one of two Southwest Regional representatives serving on the AIANTA board. I am also Executive Director of the Nevada Indian Commission and a member of the U.S. Travel and Tourism Advisory Board, advising the Secretary of Commerce.

AIANTA's professional staff and volunteer Board facilitate tribal tourism technical assistance and training and create and nurture a network of partners, including federal agencies, universities, tourism industry leaders and national Indian and non-Indian nonprofits to leverage scarce available resources. We provide these services through a cooperative agreement with the Bureau of Indian Affairs, Division of Transportation, a foremost partner from the beginning of our efforts to assist tribes. The BIA cooperative agreement is made possible by the Intermodal Surface Transportation Efficiency Act of 1991(ISTEA) and subsequent re-authorizations. With supporters in Congress, we are working to establish a permanent program with a set budget within the reauthorization of MAP–21 to continue to help tribes build their capacity for tourism development.

Capitalizing on the International Tourism

According to Department of Commerce surveys, nearly 38 million overseas tourists visited the United States in 2013 and more than 1.5 million of those travelers visited Indian Country. From 2011 to 2012, American Indian communities saw a

135 percent increase in visitors from China, a 73 percent increase from Australia and a 60 percent increase from France.

Though we do not yet have the funds to collect our own data scientifically, we monitor the growing interest in Native-run operations and reservation trips. We're seeing significant increases in travel to Indian Country.

Tourism Successes and Opportunities in Indian Country

There are more tribal tourism success stories than there is time to name them.

Standing Rock Sioux Tribe, which straddles North and South Dakota, operates hundreds of reservation tours every year. In 2013, eight Japanese visitors stayed six weeks and spent an average of $1500 a day at Standing Rock. The tribe also offers limited buffalo hunts at $10,000 per customer.

Icy Strait Point, a majority-owned Native Alaskan business, operates 21 excursions in Hoonah, Alaska, 35 miles west of Juneau. The mostly Tlingit staff accommodated 69 cruise ships in 2013.

One of AIANTA's members, Monument Valley Simpson's Trailhandler Tours, is a regular part of AIANTA's delegation to ITB Berlin, the second largest travel trade marketplace in the world. Specializing in tours of Southern Utah by Navajo guides who teach Navajo culture, the business welcomes between 80 and 100 people on an average summer night—mostly foreign tourists—and employs about 30 people year round.

Each of the members of this Committee has Indian Country success stories of their own like these back home. There is money to be made in Indian Country tourism, and when that is better understood, more investment will follow. That is why one of AIANTA's strategic goals is greater public awareness for Indian Country tourism.

To boost awareness efforts, AIANTA is building an Indian Country destinations web site to assist tribes, especially those tribes that are rural and remote. With our partner The George Washington University, we are creating web-based training courses for tribal members to earn tourism certificates. We lead delegations to world tradeshows, use social and mainstream media to tell our stories, and work with our partners on projects that recognize the achievements of America's native peoples. Name any one of two dozen national American Indian associations or national or regional tourism associations—NCAI, NIGA, NARF, Southeast Tourism Society, Western States Policy Council, the American Recreation Coalition, National Geographic Society—and we are working with them and they are supporting us in our efforts to build awareness, attract resources and encourage travel, tourism and recreation development in Indian Country. We also have a Memorandum of Understanding with the Department of the Interior, and all of its bureaus.

Answering the Question: Where will investment come from?

We look to traditional and non-traditional sources for future investment in Indian Country tourism: from the tribes themselves, from tribal entrepreneurs, from other tribes, from hospitality industry investors, from federal partners, and from foreign investors.

Our confidence comes from the recent strong interest in Native culture on many fronts. This has resulted in more tourists but also more trade, as people around the world become more aware of Indian Country goods and services. International tour companies like Tauck Inc. are adding Native attractions and Native interpretation to their itineraries. AMTRAK is talking about adding native interpretation to their western routes. Because of the data trends and the anecdotal evidence of the enormous and growing interest in native culture by the Chinese, European Union countries, Australians and others, we believe the wave of visitation from international visitors will rise at an increasingly strong pace. We also believe that if Indian Country is given a voice and is represented well in BRAND USA marketing, we can add significant value to the national travel and tourism strategy by attracting more international visitors than ever before.

Investment in Tourism Infrastructure and Capacity Building

For every success story in Indian Country tourism there is a another story of the need for infrastructure and capacity building that exists in tribal communities to truly make tourism a viable anchor for tribal economic development. Our work has opened our eyes to the enormous potential that international visitors represent for tribal tourism. We also know that most tribes do not have the capacity to handle this business and would find their communities overrun by the magnitude of people that are seeking the opportunity to visit.

The basic infrastructure improvements that tribal communities need today are the amenities that constitute a successful tourism industry. No one wants tourism to become a tool of exploitation or to negatively impact quality of life, but it can happen if our communities are not prepared. If a tribe, as a sovereign nation, chooses tourism as a means to diversify their economy and improve quality of life, AIANTA seeks to assist it with the tools and resources so they are able to manage tourism and to control the manner and timing of growth.

The first steps to attracting additional tourism investment are the ones we are taking: providing additional technical assistance and training to tribes and encouraging community inventories and feasibility studies to find the right mix of visitor businesses and services for each tribe who wants to participate in tourism. We encourage regional cooperation: tour itineraries that include the best the tribe has to offer, as well as, the best their region has to offer, on and off the reservation. We encourage revising or establishing tribal laws to protect resources, while welcoming investment. These include intellectual and cultural property laws, land use plans and zoning. We encourage the participation of youth in the development of tourism plans, projects, hospitality courses and businesses.

Congress Can Help

Without asking for any increase in any federal budget, Congress can increase Indian Country tourism development. How? By refining the language in the Highway Reauthorization Bill authorizing spending for technical assistance and training in tribal tourism and recreation and specifying an amount to be spent, AIANTA can increase delivery of these services to Indian Country resulting in tourism business development and employment growth.

Greater coordination and collaboration between Indian tourism programs and federal agencies with tourism programs, such as that outlined in legislation currently being written under the title "NATIVE Act" or the Native American Tourism and Improving Visitor Experience Act, could also boost tourism development in Indian Country without expending any additional funds.

AIANTA's bottom line is this: If the federal resources that currently exist for tourism were organized to be used collaboratively and made available to tribal governments, communities and businesses, the result would lead to more visitors, more income and more investment in Indian Country tourism.

Conclusion

Mr. Chairman and members of the Committee, I thank you for your interest in tribal tourism and AIANTA's work. I thank you for including tourism in your exploration of investment in Indian Country economic development, and invite you to call upon AIANTA in the future as a resource.

APPENDIX I—THE CASE FOR FUNDING TRIBAL TOURISM EDUCATION AND DEVELOPMENT TRAINING UNDER BUREAU OF INDIAN AFFAIRS—DIVISION OF TRANSPORTATION ADMINISTRATIVE FUNDS

For more than a decade, the American Indian Alaska Native Tourism Association (AIANTA) has been serving as the national center for providing tourism and recreational travel technical assistance and training to American Indian nations. These dynamic and expanding services have been funded through Bureau of Indian Affairs Division of Transportation (BIA–DOT) Administrative Funds under ISTEA in fulfillment of the section on Education and Training—tourism recreational travel. To sustain and enhance tribal economic development opportunities in tourism and recreational travel, the services and support—tribal tourism education, training and technical assistance—that AIANTA provides to tribes through BIA–DOT should be designated as a permanent tribal tourism program in reauthorizing legislation.

The Intermodal Surface Transportation Act of 1991 included language (unchanged through Map–21) to provide assistance to develop "tourism recreational travel to American Indian tribal governments" (see italic sections):

Education and Training program

(b) GRANTS AND CONTRACTS—The Secretary may make grants and enter into contracts for education and training, technical assistance, and related support service that will—

(3) establish, in cooperation with State transportation or highway departments and universities (A) urban technical assistance program centers in States with 2 or more urbanized areas of 50,000 to 1,000,000 population, and (B) rural technical assistance program centers. Not less than 2 centers under paragraph (3) *shall be designated to provide transportation assistance that may include, but is not necessarily limited to, a "circuit-rider" program, providing training on intergovernmental transportation planning and project selection, and tourism recreational travel to American Indian tribal governments.*

(c) FUNDS—The funds required to carry out the provisions of this section shall be taken out of administrative funds deducted under section 104(a). The sum of $6,000,000 per fiscal year for each of the fiscal years 1992, 1993, 1994, 1995, 1996, and 1997 shall be set aside from such administrative funds for the purpose of providing technical and financial support for these centers, including up to 100 percent for services provided to American Indian tribal governments.

BIA Division of Transportation

To carry out the mandate for Education and Training for tourism recreational travel for tribal governments, BIA–DOT brought tribal issues to the National Academy of Science's Transportation Research Board (TRB) in 1993 and tribal participation to the 1995 White House Conference on Tourism. Three years later, in 1998, BIA–DOT and tribal tourism leaders from across the country worked together to produce the first American Indian Tourism Conference (AITC) in Albuquerque, NM.

AIANTA

The impact of tribal and BIA involvement in the planning and execution of the Lewis and Clark Bicentennial commemoration led to formation of the American Indian Alaska Native Tourism Association (AIANTA). AIANTA's was established in 2002 to support professional tribal tourism development through education and training and promote tribal involvement in the tourism industry, including an annual American Indian Tourism Conference. AIANTA attained 501c3 status in 2009 with the mission "to define, introduce, grow and sustain American Indian Alaska Native and Native Hawaiian tourism that honors and sustains tribal traditions and values."

AIANTA/BIA Cooperative Agreement

The relationship between BIA and AIANTA continues to evolve, and AIANTA's services to Indian Country have expanded and deepened. In 2010 AIANTA and BIA signed a cooperative agreement to continue providing tribal tourism education, training and other services to tribes, with funding provided by BIA–DOT under ISTEA. Cooperative agreement funding to AIANTA in 2012 was $1.3 million, $825,000 in 2013, and $900,000 pending for 2014.

Under the cooperative agreement, AIANTA provides tribal tourism education, training and technical assistance to tribes via several ongoing program areas:

Expand Tribal Tourism Education and Training

• AIANTA continues to present the American Indian Tourism Conference, hosted each September by various American Indian and Alaska Native tribes in their homelands. The 2013 15th annual AITC was hosted by the Cherokee Nation at Catoosa, OK.

• The conference is designed to share knowledge, experience and best practices and features mobile workshops, networking events and a line-up of expert speakers and presenters. In 2012, AITC established a scholarship fund to support Native American, Alaska Native and Native Hawaiian students preparing for careers in the hospitality, tourism and culinary arts industries.

• AIANTA also supports regional tribal tourism education and development conferences in all six of its member regions, including the Native American Tourism of Wisconsin (NATOW) annual conference, the annual Alaska Heritage and Cultural Tourism Conference in Sitka and others.

Research and Develop Tribal Tourism Resources

• AIANTA works closely with the Department of Commerce, National Travel and Tourism Office, and others to make tourism research data available to members via website (*www.aianta.org*), newsletters, training sessions and other means. According to the Department of Commerce, American Indian communities saw a 46 percent increase in international visitors from 2011 to 2012, including a 135 percent increase from China, 73 percent increase from Australia and 60 percent increase from France.

Develop International Tribal Tourism Outreach

• In 2013, for the 5th consecutive year, AIANTA participated in ITB, the world's leading travel trade show held annually in Berlin, Germany. AIANTA hosted tribes and tribal enterprises from across the United States at the heavily visited Brand USA Pavilion. The event attracted more than 113,000 international tourism professionals, tour operators, travel agents, media, suppliers, buyers and destinations. At ITB 2011, AIANTA received the CBS (Cologne Business School) Best Exhibitor Award as 5th Best Exhibitor in the category of NGO's/Non-Profit Institutions.

- AIANTA collaborates with Brand USA to provide editorial content on Indian Country in the international travel guide *Discover America*, published in nine languages and distributed worldwide.

- AIANTA also participates in the U.S. Travel Association's annual IPW (formerly International Pow Wow), now in its 45th year. At IPW 2013, AIANTA conducted more than 40 business meetings with journalists, tour operators and consultants from across the globe, with strongest interest from the U.S., France, Germany, Canada and Japan. Nearly 6,400 delegates from the U.S. and 70 countries attended the event.

Form and Nurture Partnerships

- AIANTA actively collaborates with a growing network of formal and informal, public and private partners.

- To give one example, AIANTA has partnered with the National Park Service (NPS) since 2010 to develop authentic interpretation of American Indian cultural heritage landscapes, economic opportunities for Native concessionaires and tribal tourism businesses, and training and career path opportunities for NPS Native employees.

- During the 150th anniversary of America's Civil War (2011–2015), AIANTA and BIA collaborated with NPS to publish the landmark handbook, *American Indians and the Civil War.*

- In 2012, AIANTA's partnership with NPS led to formalization of a groundbreaking MOU between AIANTA and the Department of the Interior, and all DOI bureaus/agencies, for the support and enhancement of American Indian tourism.

AIANTA also actively collaborates with many private partners for:

- Development of a tribal tourism Destinations Website.

- Establishment of education and training, including certificate and degree programs in tribal tourism development with George Washington University.

- Technical assistance to tribes in developing their destinations, itineraries and customer service and for bringing authentic Native perspectives to tours that impact Indian Country with Tauck, Inc. a travel industry leader since 1925.

- International tribal tourism outreach with Brand USA

Create Tools for Tribal Tourism Development and Marketing

- In 2013, AIANTA and the National Tribal Geographic Information Support Center are collaborating to create a state of the art destinations website for tribes, to be launched in 2014.

- In conjunction with the web site, AIANTA is developing training modules in destinations development and marketing.

Raise Public Awareness of the Significance of Tribal Tourism

- In 2013, AIANTA's public awareness efforts on behalf of tribal tourism resulted in 267,815,996 media impressions and 60 countries reached via social media and the website.

National Tribal Tourism Leadership

Today AIANTA is universally recognized as a national leader of the tourism industry and is included in the President's National Travel and Tourism Strategy. In 2013, the vice-president of AIANTA's board of directors was appointed to serve on the Travel and Tourism Advisory Board, established in 2003 to act as advisory body to the Secretary of Commerce and the White House on matters relating to the travel and tourism industry in the United States. Most recently, the president of AIANTA's board was appointed to the Tourism Committee of the National Congress of American Indians.

Request

- Based on the existing funding authority, BIA–DOT's history of funding the services delivered to tribes by AIANTA, and the effectiveness of those services, AIANTA respectfully requests that these programs and their funding stream be included in reauthorization of BIA–DOT, in the annual amount of $2 million.
- Sample reauthorization language:

To be added:

A tribal technical assistance center will be established under BIA–DOT and managed by the American Indian Alaska Native Tourism Association through

a cooperative agreement to provide tourism and recreational travel training and technical assistance to American Indian tribal governments, enterprises andorganizations.
Also:
$2 million will be spent annually through BIA–DOT for the tourism program.

APPENDIX II—STATEMENT IN SUPPORT OF THE NATIVE ACT BY AMERICAN INDIAN ALASKA NATIVE TOURISM ASSOCIATION BOARD PRESIDENT SHERRY L. RUPERT

The American Indian Alaska Native Tourism Association (AIANTA) applauds Senator Brian Schatz, Chairman of the Senate Subcommittee on Tourism, Competiveness and Innovation, for the introduction of the Native American Tourism and Improving Visitor Experience (NATIVE) Act.

AIANTA wholeheartedly supports the NATIVE Act, and the AIANTA Board of Directors has endorsed it unanimously.

The NATIVE Act will accelerate Native American tourism development and increase international tourism to the U.S. According to the latest available Department of Commerce figures, from 2011 to 2012, visitors from overseas to Native American communities increased 46 percent. The number of tribes pursuing tourism is increasing, along with the need for tourism infrastructure and visitor services.

Tourism can help many tribes and native communities become more self-sufficient, create jobs and businesses, and protect tribal heritage assets while sharing tribal culture with domestic and global audiences.

The NATIVE Act will make it possible for AIANTA to accelerate the fulfillment of its mission to define, introduce, grow and sustain American Indian, Alaska Native and Native Hawaiian tourism in significant ways: expanding its tribal tourism education, training and technical assistance programs, helping develop tourism resources such as visitor asset inventories and tour itineraries, expanding its international and national visitor outreach and assisting in the development of tourism infrastructure to heighten visitor experience.

The CHAIRMAN. Thank you, Ms. Rupert. We appreciate your testimony.

I am going to start with you, Mr. Davis. Your testimony mentioned several programs that are currently authorized and will be highly successful if properly funded. Could you prioritize these programs at all? In other words, which one is the best one?

Mr. DAVIS. Thank you, Senator. Let me look through my notes here really quickly. As far as the programs that we feel have really had an impact in the community, I think the Buy Indian Act has the most potential. That is why we are calling for enforcement of the Buy Indian Act. I think if we increase the Indian loan guaranty program it would increase activity in Indian Country, economic development activity in Indian Country, procurement opportunities through program that we run and have run successfully for many years, the Procurement Technical Assistance Center, in partnership with DOD, DLA, has proven to grow.

For example, yesterday in our RES D.C. event, $200 million in contracting opportunities for American Indian businesses through Lockheed Martin. It is something that we have the opportunity to continue to grow that, and we are continuing to support those programs and ask for them to continue to be increased and paid attention to in funding out of this Committee.

The CHAIRMAN. Okay. I am going to go to you, Gerald. You had talked about, in your testimony, successful experiences in investing in Indian Country. Your testimony cites some bleak statistics about how much is needed out there, how many folks don't have access to financial institutions. A number of witnesses today have talked about or written about poor understanding by private investors when it comes to investing in Indian Country. Do you have any ideas on how we can change that?

Mr. SHERMAN. I think we mentioned some of the things in here that we would like to see that can be done here. The CDFI Fund has been a big benefit to Native CDFIs in making their programs a little more accessible in some ways and kind of tweaking them I think will help us. For instance, the new market tax credit program, we would like to see things done to maximize the flow of capital to Indian Country. I think they can look at providing leaders and reevaluate these applications who have experience in Indian Country and who understand a little bit more about it. If that is not possible, I think the staff of the Native American component at the CDFI Fund is very good and they have a good understanding and good relationship with them.

The CDFI Bond Guaranty program, which really would be a really big benefit to providing long-term, low-cost money, would work very well if they could find a way to make it better for Indian Country.

The CHAIRMAN. Thank you very much.

I have a vote that is going to close in about four minutes. Normally they extend them, and with my luck Harry would actually close it in four minutes and I would miss it. I don't want to do that.

So I am going to have to gavel out, because I am not sure any of the other members are coming back. I want to say thank you, I want to apologize then I want to say thank you. This is not the end of this discussion. Economic development is critically important, private investment as well as Federal investment in Indian Country is critically important, as we move forward.

I just want to say thank you to the witnesses for what you do for economic development in Indian Country. All five of you have an understanding of what the challenges are in Indian Country and how to best meet those challenges. If we can empower you, I think Indian Country will be a better place.

Thank you all very much. This hearing is adjourned.

[Whereupon, at 3:19 p.m., the hearing was adjourned.]

APPENDIX

PREPARED STATEMENT OF HON. BRIAN SCHATZ, U.S. SENATOR FROM HAWAII

I want to thank Chairman Tester and Vice Chairman Barrasso for holding this important hearing today on the need to encourage greater investment in Native communities and to enhance opportunities for Native enterprise development.

The diversity of our Native nations as well as the level of self-determination they exercise in the United States is found nowhere else in the world. Both domestic and international travelers have shown an increasing interest and desire to learn more about our country's indigenous cultures. Native communities have the opportunity to showcase their culture and offer authentic and unique products and services that both domestic and international consumers will value. Native entrepreneurs and business owners have the capacity to contribute significantly to America's economic growth, while also improving the socio-economic conditions and advancing self-sufficiency in American Indian, Alaska Native, and Native Hawaiian communities. Federal efforts and programs that exist today must be maintained and improved to enhance economic opportunities for Native communities.

To illuminate the positive results of increased credit accessibility and support for economic growth in Native communities, we can look to the Small Business Administration (SBA) 8(a) Business Development Program. Native participation in federal contracting through the SBA 8(a) program has supported small businesses and strengthened Native economies. New businesses that are created benefit Native communities and jumpstart a positive cycle of capital flows. Native communities may also find business incentives to preserve their cultures, traditions, languages, and customary ways of life. In return, Native enterprises have also provided quality services and products to the Federal Government and to the commercial markets.

I also understand that cultural and heritage assets are particularly valuable in the tourism industry. The $180 billion tourism industry is America's number one service export, and President Obama has set a goal of attracting 100 million international visitors annually by 2021. To advance this National Travel and Tourism Strategy, expanding heritage and cultural tourism opportunities will spur economic growth, create jobs, and increase tourism revenues. That is why I have developed a draft Native American Tourism and Improving Visitor Experience (NATIVE) Act. The NATIVE Act will empower Native communities to share their culture and tell their own stories; enhance and integrate Native American tourism into our national tourism strategy; and increase coordination and collaboration between federal tourism assets. In addition, new infrastructure needed to attract and sustain tourism will elevate living standards in Native communities. The unrealized potential for Native tourism will yield substantial benefits to the U.S. economy and to Native communities.

I look forward to continuing to work with the witnesses to advance economic development, spur job creation, uplift Native communities and help Native families build a better future for their children.

———

PREPARED STATEMENT OF ROWENA AKANA, TRUSTEE, OFFICE OF HAWAIIAN AFFAIRS

Native American Tourism and Improving Visitor Experience (NATIVE) Act

Thank you for allowing me to officer testimony on the proposed Native American Tourism and Improving Visitor Experience (NATIVE) Act. As a Native Hawaiian, I am in support of the NATIVE Act.

I serve as one of nine elected trustees for the Office of Hawaiian Affairs (OHA). OHA's mission is to advocate for our Native Hawaiian beneficiaries and to malama (protect) Hawai'i's environmental resources and cultural assets. We work to better the conditions of our Native Hawaiian beneficiaries, to perpetuate Native Hawaiian culture, and to protect Native Hawaiian entitlements. Our goal is to build a strong and healthy Hawaiian nation, recognized both nationally and internationally.

For as long as I can remember, Hawaii has been marketed as a great tourist destination. However, the marketing done by the State of Hawaii features beautiful beaches, surf, Hula girls and other commercial advertisement.

This year, for the very first time, the Office of Hawaiian Affairs will be focusing on marketing authentic Hawaiian experiences and using Native Hawaiian vendors to promote economic development and enterprise for Native Hawaiians.

The idea is not new, however, because individual vendors did not have the financial resources or the marketing expertise to promote their businesses, the idea remained just an idea.

Authentic Native Hawaiian activities such as exploring pristine rainforests; identifying medicinal indigenous plants with healing properties; and visiting the only royal palace in the Unites States where our king and queen ruled the lands during the Kingdom of Hawaii are just some of the ways that visitors can experience our true Hawaiian history. There are many Native Hawaiian activities that general visitors never get to visit. This is a shame since there is so much more they can learn about Native Hawaiian culture, traditions and practices.

I believe that passing this piece of legislation is necessary to accomplish the goals of all Native Americans to boost their economic development objectives, while at the same time introducing the general public to Native cultures, history, and practices.

PREPARED STATEMENT OF MARK AZURE, PRESIDENT, FORT BELKNAP INDIAN COMMUNITY COUNCIL

TRIBAL ONLINE LENDING: STRENGTHENING SELF-SUFFICIENCY FOR ISOLATED TRIBES

The Fort Belknap Indian Community Council welcomes the opportunity to submit this written testimony for the Senate Committee on Indian Affairs ("Committee") hearing record on the vitally important issue of encouraging investment for economic development in Indian country.

At your hearing on June 25, 2014, the Committee heard testimony on the challenges and opportunities for economic development in Indian country. On the Fort Belknap Indian Reservation we know that a self-sufficient community is critical to a healthy economy, but the reality is many Native communities continue to struggle with remoteness, limited infrastructure, and access to capital. Our Tribe has worked to foster economic growth despite these challenges. We have encouraged economic development through strong leadership, collective goal setting and visioning to successfully overcome these historic challenges. Our hope is that the Tribe's testimony can highlight a successful economic venture in Indian country that can be useful and informative to the Committee.

Economic Development on Isolated Reservations

The Fort Belknap Indian Reservation is geographically isolated. Our homeland to both the Gros Ventre (Aaniiih) and the Assiniboine (Nakoda) Tribes is located in North Central Montana, forty miles south of the Canadian border and twenty miles north of the Missouri River, several hours from the nearest metropolitan areas in Great Falls and Billings.

The Fort Belknap Indian Reservation encompasses a large area consisting of 675,147 acres. The main industry is agriculture, consisting of small cattle ranches, raising alfalfa hay for feed and larger dry land farms. Fort Belknap has a tribal membership of approximately 7,000 enrolled members, with a median income of less than $12,000 each.

Like many isolated rural reservations, it is difficult to grow local businesses sufficient to support the needs of our 7,000 tribal members. In 2009, to encourage investment and strength self-sufficiency opportunities, the Tribe created an economic development holding company, the Island Mountain Development Group (IMDG).

The IMDG is dedicated to serving the Gros Ventre and Assiniboine Nations by creating a self-sustaining, local economy through the creation of business opportunities, jobs, workplace training, positive role models, and resource development. As such, the IMDG quest is to go well beyond simply being able to open businesses and create jobs. Rather, they must strengthen our communities by advancing the overall well-being of our people. In the development of the Tribe's online lending enterprises, we have found a successful economic development venture that is sustainable and maximizes the assets of our community.

Ft. Belknap's Tribal Lending Operations

Pursuant to tribal law, Ft. Belknap has developed online consumer lending enterprises whereby we make small-denomination, short-term installment loans to consumers around the country via the Internet. Our lending businesses have become an important economic driver on the Reservation.

Ft. Belknap employs more than 30 full-time employees in our two call center locations on the Reservation, which serve our online lending businesses. Employees assist in loan verification and loan processing. In this collaborative environment, they receive general computer training, development of their customer service skills, and support in life/work balance that allow them to prepare for a successful future and further take their careers to the next level. Our call centers focus their hiring directly from our tribal college. The call centers are supported by dozens more IMDG employees who also have roles in management, marketing, compliance and other areas essential to running our online consumer lending portfolios. Our tribal employees are excellent at what they do. They are empathetic, they are professional, and they enjoy being able to help good people in difficult situations.

Similarly, our loyal customers are hard-working folks with verifiable employment and bank accounts, and most important, a demonstrated capacity to repay. The Tribe offers financial products that our customers cannot access from traditional financial institutions. We successfully serve an important market need. In fact, the majority of our customers are unable to get loans from traditional banks. As Indian people, we understand this frustration. In response, the Tribe has created a good product that is designed to take chances on higher-risk customers. Our customers are neither desperate nor ignorant; they understand they are using an expensive form of borrowing, but they chose the convenience of our services. As they repay their small loans with us, our customers earn better and better interest rates, and we help rebuild their credit ratings.

Tribal Online Lending = Essential Tribal Income

The Tribe has discovered that e-commerce is one of the few industries that can truly thrive on an isolated, rural reservation such as ours. Today approximately 70 people are employed by IMDG overall, with more than $1.4M annually in payroll paid to our local employees. Approximately 20 percent of Ft. Belknap's revenue is now generated through our government-owned companies. The Tribe has been able to take the profits from our lending companies and reinvest them and diversify our economy.

The income has allowed us to create:

- Snake Butte Construction
- Smokehouse Grille and Trading Post
- Little River Smokehouse
- Fort Belknap Tourism
- Spirit Box Technologies
- Smokehouse Coffee House

Funded entirely by our lending enterprises, we will be opening a grocery co-op this summer in an area of the Ft. Belknap Reservation that is a food desert.

Early Attacks Against Gaming—Same as Against Tribal Online Lending

Nearly every economic endeavor that has proved viable for Indian tribes comes under aggressive attack—tobacco, gas, gaming and now, online lending. Gaming has been one of the few truly successful economic development industries for Indian Country. Unfortunately that success has not reached most of the more rural and isolated reservations, such as Ft. Belknap. Gaming is a local population-based industry. Therefore, most of that revenue is generated by tribes located closer to urban populations. For more geographically-isolated tribes like Ft. Belknap, large income-producing gaming operations are not realistic.

Almost all the same arguments made against Indian gaming 25 years ago are the same arguments that are being made against online lending today:

- Tribes are trying to skirt state laws.
- Tribes are avoiding state taxes.
- The industry is unsavory; Tribes need to be protected.
- Finance partners make all the money; Tribes will never reap the benefits.
- The industry takes advantage of people of limited economic means who cannot be trusted to make their own decisions.

All of the arguments are wrong. Today, Tribes have proven every argument hollow.

Tribes are fully capable of choosing our business partners and making smart business deals. As is universally true, almost no business starts up in Indian Country without borrowing from outside sources or building capacity with outside partners.

However, as with the gaming industry, we are gaining that experience and expertise through strong, smart partnerships.

Tribes are fully capable of regulating our own industries. And most importantly, Tribes are not avoiding state laws; we are implementing tribal laws. Tribes are fully capable of running our own businesses, regulating our own commerce, and being fair to consumers.

Ft. Belknap Tribal regulations require: meaningful underwriting (including verifiable employment and bank account and demonstrated ability to repay); compliance with Ft. Belknap's own strict consumer protection requirements; and compliance with all federal laws. While there is no federal interest rate regulation, there are more than a dozen other federal laws with which our businesses must comply, required to do so by tribal law.

Conclusion

Fort Belknap Indian Community Council is working to improve the economic conditions for our people and create jobs in our communities. E-commerce and online lending offers us a glimmer of hope that strengthens our self-sufficiency. While each Tribal community is unique, our Tribe believes we have a success story to share with others looking to spur economic development in Indian country.

For your information, there is an article from the April 2014 issue of The Federal Lawyer (*http://www.bestlawyers.com/Downloads/Articles/4218—1.pdf*) which sets forth a lot of the legal and historical background for our online businesses. I hope you will read it and will want to learn more. I also hope I might have the chance in the future to tell you more about our online lending businesses and all the good they are doing for our customers and for our humble Ft. Belknap Indian Community.

Thank you for your consideration of my testimony and find below three recommended actions for the Committee's further consideration.

Recommendations

(1) Conduct SCIA Hearing to Discuss Tribal Online Lending and Learn More about This Important Opportunity for Indian Country

(2) Acknowledge and Encourage Tribal Lending Best Practices and Regulatory Development

(3) Acknowledge and Encourage the Tribal Lending Industry's Access to National Banking System and Payment-Processing Network

www.ingramcontent.com/pod-product-compliance
Lightning Source LLC
Chambersburg PA
CBHW080555290526
45790CB00006B/2656